ta Learning

with Python

Meta learning using one-shot learning, MAML, Reptile, and
Meta-SGD with TensorFlow

Sudharsan Ravichandiran

BIRMINGHAM - MUMBAI

Hands-On Meta Learning with Python

Commissioning Editor: Pavan Ramchandani
Acquisition Editor: Pavan Ramchandani
Content Development Editor: Chris D'cruz
Technical Editor: Dinesh Pawar
Copy Editor: Safis Editing
Project Coordinator: Namrata Swetta
Proofreader: Safis Editing
Indexer: Tejal Daruwale Soni
Graphics: Tom Scaria
Production Coordinator: Nilesh Mohite

First published: December 2018

Production reference: 1261218

Published by Packt Publishing Ltd.
Livery Place
35 Livery Street
Birmingham
B3 2PB, UK.

ISBN 978-1-78953-420-7

www.packtpub.com

To my adorable Mom, Kasthury, and to my beloved Dad, Ravichandiran.

- Sudharsan Ravichandiran

`mapt.io`

Mapt is an online digital library that gives you full access to over 5,000 books and videos, as well as industry leading tools to help you plan your personal development and advance your career. For more information, please visit our website.

Why subscribe?

- Spend less time learning and more time coding with practical eBooks and videos from over 4,000 industry professionals

- Improve your learning with Skill Plans built especially for you

- Get a free eBook or video every month

- Mapt is fully searchable

- Copy and paste, print, and bookmark content

Packt.com

Did you know that Packt offers eBook versions of every book published, with PDF and ePub files available? You can upgrade to the eBook version at `www.packt.com` and as a print book customer, you are entitled to a discount on the eBook copy. Get in touch with us at `customercare@packtpub.com` for more details.

At `www.packt.com`, you can also read a collection of free technical articles, sign up for a range of free newsletters, and receive exclusive discounts and offers on Packt books and eBooks.

Contributors

About the author

Sudharsan Ravichandiran is a data scientist, researcher, artificial intelligence enthusiast, and YouTuber (search for `Sudharsan reinforcement learning`). He completed his bachelor's in information technology at Anna University. His area of research focuses on practical implementations of deep learning and reinforcement learning, which includes natural language processing and computer vision. He is an open source contributor and loves answering questions on Stack Overflow. He also authored a best-seller, *Hands-On Reinforcement Learning with Python*, published by Packt Publishing.

I would like to thank my amazing parents and my brother, Karthikeyan, for inspiring and motivating me. My big thanks to my best friend, Nikhil Aditya. Huge thanks to Veena Pagare for giving me an amazing opportunity. Special thanks to my dear friend, Sri Hari Charan, who shaped my life. I can't thank enough my best friend, Gautham, for cheering me up through all my tough times, and I am forever grateful to My Soeor, who always has my back.

About the reviewers

Gautham Krishna Gudur is a machine learning engineer and researcher working on extracting actionable insights in healthcare (medical wearables) using artificial intelligence. He also does independent research at the intersection of applied machine learning/deep learning, physical activity sensing using sensors and wearable data, computer vision, and ubiquitous computing. Previously, he was a research assistant in the areas of gesture recognition, data science, and IoT at Chennai, India. He actively contributes to the research community by authoring and presenting research publications at renowned conferences around the world. During his undergraduate study, he was also an avid competitive programmer on online platforms such as HackerRank.

Armando Fandango creates AI-empowered products by leveraging his expertise in deep learning, machine learning, distributed computing, and computational methods, and has fulfilled thought-leadership roles as Chief Data Scientist and Director at start-ups and large enterprises. He has been advising high-tech AI-based start-ups. Armando has authored books titled *Python Data Analysis - Second Edition* and *Mastering TensorFlow*. He has also published research in international journals and conferences.

Packt is searching for authors like you

If you're interested in becoming an author for Packt, please visit `authors.packtpub.com` and apply today. We have worked with thousands of developers and tech professionals, just like you, to help them share their insight with the global tech community. You can make a general application, apply for a specific hot topic that we are recruiting an author for, or submit your own idea.

Table of Contents

Preface

Hands-On Meta Learning with Python explains the fundamentals of meta learning and helps you to understand the concept of learning to learn. You will go through various one-shot learning algorithms, such as siamese, prototypical, relation, and memory-augmented networks, and implement them in TensorFlow and Keras. You will also learn about the state-of-the-art meta learning algorithms, such as model-agnostic meta learning (MAML), Reptile, and fast context adaptation via meta learning (CAML). You will then explore how to learn quickly with meta-SGD and discover how to perform unsupervised learning using meta learning.

Who this book is for

This book will help machine learning enthusiasts, AI researchers, and data scientists who want to learn about meta learning as an advanced approach for training machine learning models. The book assumes a working knowledge of machine learning concepts and a sound knowledge of Python programming.

What this book covers

Chapter 1, *Introduction to Meta Learning*, helps us to understand what meta learning is and covers the different types of meta learning. We will also learn how meta learning uses few-shot learning by learning from a few data points. We will then see how to become familiar with gradient descent. Later in the chapter, we will see optimization as a model for the few shot learning setting.

Chapter 2, *Face and Audio Recognition Using Siamese Networks*, starts by explaining what siamese networks are and how siamese networks are used in the one-shot learning setting. We will look at the architecture of a siamese network and some of the applications of a siamese network. Then, we will see how to use the siamese networks to build face and audio recognition models.

Chapter 3, *Prototypical Networks and Their Variants*, explains what prototypical networks are and how they are used in the few shot learning scenario. We will see how to build a prototypical network to perform classification on an omniglot character set. Later in the chapter, we will look at different variants of prototypical networks, such as the Gaussian prototypical networks and semi-prototypical networks.

Chapter 4, *Relation and Matching Networks Using TensorFlow,* helps us to understand the relation network architecture and how relation network is used in one-shot, few-shot, and zero-shot learning settings. We will then see how to build a relation network using TensorFlow. Next, we will learn about the matching network and its architecture. We will also explore full contextual embeddings and how to build a matching network using TensorFlow.

Chapter 5, *Memory-Augmented Neural Networks,* covers what neural Turing machines (NTMs) are and how they make use of external memory for storing and retrieving information. We will look at different addressing mechanisms used in NTMs and then we will learn about memory augmented neural networks and how they differ from the NTM architecture.

Chapter 6, *MAML and Its Variants,* deals with one of the popular meta learning algorithms, called model-agnostic meta learning (MAML). We will explore what MAML is and how it is used in supervised and reinforcement learning settings. We will also see how to build MAML from scratch. Then, we will learn about adversarial meta learning and CAML, which is used for fast context adaptation in meta learning.

Chapter 7, *Meta-SGD and Reptile,* explain how meta-SGD is used to learn all the ingredients of gradient descent algorithms, such as initial weights, learning rates, and the update direction. We will see how to build meta-SGD from scratch. Later in the chapter, we will learn about the reptile algorithm and see how it serves as an improvement over MAML. We will also see how to use the reptile algorithm for sine wave regression.

Chapter 8, *Gradient Agreement as an Optimization Objective,* covers how we can use gradient agreement as an optimization objective in the meta learning setting. We will learn what gradient agreement is and how it can enhance meta learning algorithms. Later in the chapter, we will learn how to build a gradient agreement algorithm from scratch.

Chapter 9, *Recent Advancements and Next Steps,* starts by explaining task-agnostic meta learning, and then we will see how meta learning is used in an imitation learning setting. Then, we will learn how we can apply MAML in an unsupervised learning setting using the CACTUs algorithm. Then, we will explore a deep meta learning algorithm called learning to learn in the concept space.

To get the most out of this book

You need the following software for this book:

- Python
- Anaconda
- TensorFlow
- Keras

Download the example code files

You can download the example code files for this book from your account at `www.packt.com`. If you purchased this book elsewhere, you can visit `www.packt.com/support` and register to have the files emailed directly to you.

You can download the code files by following these steps:

1. Log in or register at `www.packt.com`.
2. Select the **SUPPORT** tab.
3. Click on **Code Downloads & Errata**.
4. Enter the name of the book in the **Search** box and follow the onscreen instructions.

Once the file is downloaded, please make sure that you unzip or extract the folder using the latest version of:

- WinRAR/7-Zip for Windows
- Zipeg/iZip/UnRarX for Mac
- 7-Zip/PeaZip for Linux

The code bundle for the book is also hosted on GitHub at `https://github.com/PacktPublishing/Hands-On-Meta-Learning-with-Python`. In case there's an update to the code, it will be updated on the existing GitHub repository.

We also have other code bundles from our rich catalog of books and videos available at `https://github.com/PacktPublishing/`. Check them out!

Conventions used

There are a number of text conventions used throughout this book.

`CodeInText`: Indicates code words in text, database table names, folder names, filenames, file extensions, pathnames, dummy URLs, user input, and Twitter handles. Here is an example: "The `read_image` function takes an image as input and returns a NumPy array."

A block of code is set as follows:

```
import re
import numpy as np
from PIL import Image
```

Bold: Indicates a new term, an important word, or words that you see onscreen.

Warnings or important notes appear like this.

Tips and tricks appear like this.

Get in touch

Feedback from our readers is always welcome.

General feedback: If you have questions about any aspect of this book, mention the book title in the subject of your message and email us at `customercare@packtpub.com`.

Errata: Although we have taken every care to ensure the accuracy of our content, mistakes do happen. If you have found a mistake in this book, we would be grateful if you would report this to us. Please visit `www.packt.com/submit-errata`, selecting your book, clicking on the Errata Submission Form link, and entering the details.

Piracy: If you come across any illegal copies of our works in any form on the internet, we would be grateful if you would provide us with the location address or website name. Please contact us at copyright@packt.com with a link to the material.

If you are interested in becoming an author: If there is a topic that you have expertise in and you are interested in either writing or contributing to a book, please visit authors.packtpub.com.

Reviews

Please leave a review. Once you have read and used this book, why not leave a review on the site that you purchased it from? Potential readers can then see and use your unbiased opinion to make purchase decisions, we at Packt can understand what you think about our products, and our authors can see your feedback on their book. Thank you!

For more information about Packt, please visit packt.com.

Introduction to Meta Learning

1

Meta learning is one of the most promising and trending research areas in the field of artificial intelligence right now. It is believed to be a stepping stone for attaining **Artificial General Intelligence** (**AGI**). In this chapter, we will learn about what meta learning is and why meta learning is the most exhilarating research in artificial intelligence right now. We will understand what is few-shot, one-shot, and zero-shot learning and how it is used in meta learning. We will also learn about different types of meta learning techniques. We will then explore the concept of learning to learn gradient descent by gradient descent where we understand how we can learn the gradient descent optimization using the meta learner. Going ahead, we will also learn about optimization as a model for few-shot learning where we will see how we can use meta learner as an optimization algorithm in the few-shot learning setting.

In this chapter, you will learn about the following:

- Meta learning
- Meta learning and few-shot
- Types of meta learning
- Learning to learn gradient descent by gradient descent
- Optimization as a model for few-shot learning

Meta learning

Meta learning is an exhilarating research domain in the field of AI right now. With plenty of research papers and advancements, meta learning is clearly making a major breakthrough in AI. Before getting into meta learning, let's see how our current AI model works.

Deep learning has progressed rapidly in recent years with great algorithms such as generative adversarial networks and capsule networks. But the problem with deep neural networks is that we need to have a large training set to train our model and it will fail abruptly when we have very few data points. Let's say we trained a deep learning model to perform task A. Now, when we have a new task, B, that is closely related to A, we can't use the same model. We need to train the model from scratch for task B. So, for each task, we need to train the model from scratch although they might be related.

Is deep learning really the true AI? Well, it is not. How do we humans learn? We generalize our learning to multiple concepts and learn from there. But current learning algorithms master only one task. Here is where meta learning comes in. Meta learning produces a versatile AI model that can learn to perform various tasks without having to train them from scratch. We train our meta learning model on various related tasks with few data points, so for a new related task, it can make use of the learning obtained from the previous tasks and we don't have to train them from scratch. Many researchers and scientists believe that meta learning can get us closer to achieving AGI. We will learn exactly how meta learning models learn the learning process in the upcoming sections.

Meta learning and few-shot

Learning from fewer data points is called **few-shot learning** or **k-shot learning** where k denotes the number of data points in each of the classes in the dataset. Let's say we are performing the image classification of dogs and cats. If we have exactly one dog and one cat image then it is called **one-shot learning**, that is, we are learning from just one data point per class. If we have, say 10 images of a dog and 10 images of a cat, then that is called 10-shot learning. So k in k-shot learning implies a number of data points we have per class. There is also **zero-shot learning** where we don't have any data points per class. Wait. What? How can we learn when there are no data points at all? In this case, we will not have data points, but we will have meta information about each of the classes and we will learn from the meta information. Since we have two classes in our dataset, that is, dog and cat, we can call it two-way k-shot learning; so n-way means the number of classes we have in our dataset.

In order to make our model learn from a few data points, we will train them in the same way. So, when we have a dataset, D, we sample a few data points from each of the classes present in our data set and we call it as **support set.** Similarly, we sample some different data points from each of the classes and call it as **query set.** So we train our model with a support set and test with a query set. We train our model in an **episodic fashion**—that is, in each episode, we sample a few data points from our dataset, D, prepare our support set and query set, and train on the support set and test on the query set. So, over series of episodes, our model will learn how to learn from a smaller dataset. We will explore this in more detail in the upcoming chapters.

Types of meta learning

Meta learning can be categorized in several ways, right from finding the optimal sets of weights to learning the optimizer. We will categorize meta learning into the following three categories:

- Learning the metric space
- Learning the initializations
- Learning the optimizer

Learning the metric space

In the metric-based meta learning setting, we will learn the appropriate metric space. Let's say we want to learn the similarity between two images. In the metric-based setting, we use a simple neural network that extracts the features from two images and finds the similarity by computing the distance between features of these two images. This approach is widely used in a few-shot learning setting where we don't have many data points. In the upcoming chapters, we will learn about metric-based learning algorithms such as Siamese networks, prototypical networks, and relation networks.

Learning the initializations

In this method, we try to learn optimal initial parameter values. What do we mean by that? Let's say we are a building a neural network to classify images. First, we initialize random weights, calculate loss, and minimize the loss through a gradient descent. So, we will find the optimal weights through gradient descent and minimize the loss. Instead of initializing the weights randomly, if can we initialize the weights with optimal values or close to optimal values, then we can attain the convergence faster and we can learn very quickly. We will see how exactly we can find these optimal initial weights with algorithms such as MAML, Reptile, and Meta-SGD in the upcoming chapters.

Learning the optimizer

In this method, we try to learn the optimizer. How do we generally optimize our neural network? We optimize our neural network by training on a large dataset and minimize the loss using gradient descent. But in the few-shot learning setting, gradient descent fails as we will have a smaller dataset. So, in this case, we will learn the optimizer itself. We will have two networks: a base network that actually tries to learn and a meta network that optimizes the base network. We will explore how exactly this works in the upcoming sections.

Learning to learn gradient descent by gradient descent

Now, we will see one of the interesting meta learning algorithms called learning to learn gradient descent by gradient descent. Isn't the name kind of daunting? Well, in fact, it is one of the simplest meta learning algorithms. We know that, in meta learning, our goal is to learn the learning process. In general, how do we train our neural networks? We train our network by computing loss and minimizing the loss through gradient descent. So, we optimize our model using gradient descent. Instead of using gradient descent can we learn this optimization process automatically?

But how can we learn this? We replace our traditional optimizer (gradient descent) with the **Recurrent Neural Network (RNN)**. But how does this work? How can we replace gradient descent with RNN? If you examine closely, what are we really doing in gradient descent? It is basically a sequence of updates from the output layer to the input layer and we store these updates in a state. So, we can use RNN and store the updates in an RNN cell.

So, the main idea of this algorithm is to replace gradient descent with RNN. But the question is how do RNNs learn? How can we optimize the RNN? For optimizing an RNN, we use gradient descent. **So, in a nutshell, we are learning to perform gradient descent through an RNN and that RNN is optimized by gradient descent and that's what is meant by the name learning to learn gradient descent by gradient descent.**

We call our RNN, an optimizer and our base network, an optimizee. Let's say we have a model f parameterized by some parameter θ. We need to find this optimal parameter θ, so that we can minimize the loss. In general, we find this optimal parameter through gradient descent, but now we use the RNN for finding this optimal parameter. So the RNN (optimizer) finds the optimal parameter and sends it to the optimizee (base network); the optimizee uses this parameter, computes the loss, and sends the loss to the RNN. Based on the loss, the RNN optimizes itself through gradient descent and updates the model parameter θ.

Confusing? Look at the following diagram: our optimizee (base network) is optimized through our optimizer (RNN). The optimizer sends the updated parameters—that is, weights—to the optimizee and the optimizee uses these weights, calculates the loss, and sends the loss to the optimizer; based on the loss, the optimizer improves itself through gradient descent:

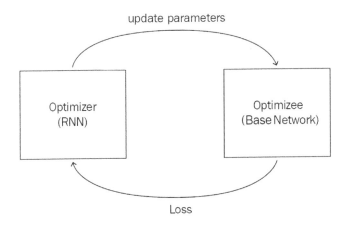

Let's say our base network (optimizee) is parameterized by θ and our RNN (optimizer) is parameterized by ϕ. What is the loss function of the optimizer? We know that the optimizer's role (RNN) is to reduce the loss of the optimizee (base network). So the loss of our optimizer is the average loss of the optimizee and it can be represented as follows:

$$L(\phi) = \mathbb{E}_f[f(\theta(f, \phi))]$$

How do we minimize this loss? We minimize this loss through gradient descent by finding the right ϕ. Okay, what does the RNN take as input and what output would it return? Our optimizer, that is, our RNN, takes as input the gradient of optimizee ∇_t as well as its previous state h_t and returns output, an update g_t that can minimize the loss of our optimizee. Let's denote our RNN by a function m:

$$(g_t, h_{t+1}) = m(\nabla_t, h_t, \phi)$$

In the previous equation, the following applies:

- ∇_t is the gradient of our model (optimizee) f, that is, $\nabla_t = \nabla_t f(\theta_t)$
- h_t is the hidden state of the RNN
- ϕ is the parameter for the RNN
- Outputs g_t and h_{t+1} is the update and next state of the RNN respectively

So, we update our model parameter values using $\theta_{t+1} = \theta_t + g_t$.

As you can see in the following diagram, our optimizer m at a time t, takes in a hidden state h_t and a gradient of θ_t as ∇_t as inputs, computes g_t and sends it to our optimizee, where it is added with θ_t and becomes θ_{t+1} for an update at the next time step:

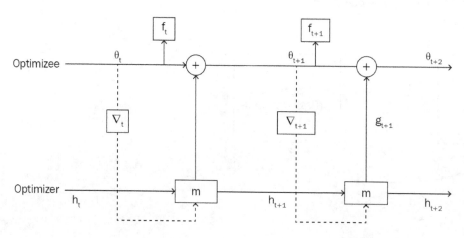

So, in this way, we learn the gradient descent optimization through gradient descent.

Optimization as a model for few-shot learning

We know that, in few-shot learning, we learn from lesser data points, but how can we apply gradient descent in a few-shot learning setting? In a few-shot learning setting, gradient descent fails abruptly due to very few data points. Gradient descent optimization requires more data points to reach the convergence and minimize loss. So, we need a better optimization technique in the few-shot regime. Let's say we have a f model parameterized by some parameter θ. We initialize this parameter θ with some random values and try to find the optimal value using gradient descent. Let's recall the update equation of our gradient descent:

$$\theta_t = \theta_{t-1} - \alpha_t \nabla_{\theta_{t-1}} L_t$$

In the previous equation, the following applies:

- θ_t is the updated parameter
- θ_{t-1} is the parameter value at previous time step
- α_t is the learning rate
- $\nabla_{\theta_{t-1}} L_t$ is the gradient of loss function with respect to θ_{t-1}

Doesn't the update equation of gradient descent look familiar? Yes, you guessed it right: it resembles the cell state update equation of LSTM and it can be written as follows:

$$c_t = f_t \odot c_{t-1} + i_t \odot \tilde{c}_t$$

We can totally relate our LSTM cell update equation with gradient descent as, let's say $f_t = 1$, then the following applies:

$$c_{t-1} = \theta_{t-1}$$

$$i_t = \alpha_t$$

$$\tilde{c}_t = \nabla_{\theta_{t-1}} L_t$$

So, instead of using gradient descent as an optimizer in the few-shot learning regime, we can use LSTM as an optimizer. Our meta learner is the LSTM, which learns the update rule for training our model. So we use two networks: one, our base learner, which learns to perform a task, and the other, the meta learner, which tries to find the optimal parameter. But how does this work?

We know that, in LSTM, we use a forget gate for discarding information that is not required in the memory, and it can be represented as follows:

$$f_t = \sigma(W_f.[h_{t-1}, x_t] + b_f)$$

How can this forget gate be useful in our optimization setting? Let's say we are in a position where the loss is high, and the gradient is close to zero. How can we escape from this position? In this case, we can shrink the parameters of our model and forget some parts of its previous value. So, we can use our forget gate to do that and it takes a current parameter value θ_{t-1}, current loss L_t, current gradient $\nabla_{\theta_{t-1}}$ and the previous forget gate as the input; it can be represented as follows:

$$f_t = \sigma(W_f.[\theta_{t-1}, l_t, \nabla_{\theta_{t-1}}, f_{t-1}] + b_f)$$

Now let's come to the input gate. We know that the input gate in LSTM is used for deciding what value to update, and it can be represented as follows:

$$i_t = \sigma(W_i.[h_{t-1}, x_t] + b_i)$$

In our few-shot learning setting, we can use this input gate to tune our learning rate to learn quickly while preventing it from divergence:

$$i_t = \sigma(W_i.[\theta_{t-1}, l_t, \nabla_{\theta_{t-1}}, i_{t-1}] + b_i)$$

So, our meta learner learns the optimal value of i_t and f_t after several updates.

But still, how does this work?

Let's say we have a base network M parameterized by θ and our LSTM meta learner R parameterized by ϕ. Assume that we have a dataset D. We split our dataset as D^{train} and D^{test} for training and testing respectively. First, we randomly initialize our meta learner parameter ϕ.

For some T number of iterations, we randomly sample data points from D^{train}, calculate the loss, and then we calculate the gradients of loss with respect to our model parameter θ. Now we feed this gradient, loss, and meta learner parameter ϕ to our meta learner. Our meta learner R will return a cell state c_t and then we update our base network M parameter θ_t at a time t as c_t. We repeat this for some N number of times, as shown in the following diagram:

```
for  t=1....T  do

            X ,Y   ⟵  Sample random batch from D^train
             t  t

            Loss   ⟵  L (M(X ; θ    ),Y )
                t            t   t-1    t

            Cell state (C )  ⟵  R((∇      Loss ,Loss ),φ)
                         t            θ        t     t
                                       t-1

            θ   ⟵  C
             t      t

end for
```

So, after T iterations, we will have an optimal parameter θ_T. But how can we check the performance of θ_T and how can we update our meta learner parameter? We take the test set and compute the loss on our test set with parameter θ_T. Then, we calculate the gradients of the loss with respect to our meta learner parameter ϕ and then we update ϕ, as shown here:

```
X,Y    ⟵  D^test

Loss      ⟵  L(M(X ; θ ),Y)
    test              T

update φ using ∇   Loss
                φ      test
```

We do this for some n number of iterations and update our meta learner. The overall algorithm is shown here:

$\phi_0 \leftarrow$ Initialize randomly

for d=1...n do

$D^{train}, D^{test} \leftarrow$ Random sample from dataset D

$\theta_0 \leftarrow C_0$

for t=1...T do

$X_t, Y_t \leftarrow$ Sample random batch from D^{train}

$Loss_t \leftarrow L(M(x_t ; \theta_{t-1}), Y_t)$

cell state $(c_t) \leftarrow R((\nabla_{\theta_{t-1}} Loss_t, Loss_t), \phi_{d-1})$

$\theta_t \leftarrow c_t$

end for

$X, Y \leftarrow D^{test}$

$Loss_{test} \leftarrow L(M(X ; \theta_T), Y_t)$

update ϕ_d using $\nabla_{\theta_{t-1}} Loss_{test}$

end for

Summary

We started off by understanding what meta learning is and how one-shot, few-shot, and zero-shot learning is used in meta learning. We learned that the support set and query set are more like a train set and test set but with k data points in each of the classes. We also saw what n-way k-shot means. Later, we understood different types of meta learning techniques. Then, we explored learning to learn gradient descent by gradient descent where we saw how RNN is used as an optimizer to optimize the base network. Later, we saw optimization as a model for few-shot learning where we used LSTM as a meta learner for optimizing in the few-shot learning setting.

In the next chapter, we will learn about a metric-based meta learning algorithm called the Siamese network and we will see how to use a Siamese network for performing face and audio recognition.

Questions

1. What is meta learning?
2. What is few-shot learning?
3. What is a support set?
4. What is a query set?
5. What is metric-based learning called?
6. How do we perform training in meta learning?

Further reading

- Learning to learn gradient descent by gradient descent: `https://arxiv.org/pdf/1606.04474.pdf`
- Optimization as a model for few-shot learning setting: `https://openreview.net/pdf?id=rJY0-Kcll`

2
Face and Audio Recognition Using Siamese Networks

In the last chapter, we learned about what meta learning is and different types of meta learning techniques. We also saw how to learn gradient descent by gradient descent and optimization as a model for few-shot learning. In this chapter, we will learn one of the most commonly used metric-based one-shot learning algorithms called **siamese networks**. We will see how siamese networks learn from very few data points and how they are used to solve the low data problem. After that we will explore the architecture of siamese networks in detail and we will see some of the applications of siamese networks. At the end of this chapter, we will learn how to build face and audio recognition models using siamese networks.

In this chapter, you will learn the following:

- What are siamese networks?
- Architecture of siamese networks
- Applications of siamese networks
- Face recognition using siamese networks
- Building an audio recognition model using siamese networks

What are siamese networks?

A siamese network is a special type of neural network and it is one of the simplest and most popularly used one-shot learning algorithms. As we have learned in the previous chapter, one-shot learning is a technique where we learn from only one training example per class. So, a siamese network is predominantly used in applications where we don't have many data points in each class. For instance, let's say we want to build a face recognition model for our organization and about 500 people are working in our organization. If we want to build our face recognition model using a **Convolutional Neural Network** (**CNN**) from scratch, then we need many images of all of these 500 people for training the network and attaining good accuracy. But apparently, we will not have many images for all of these 500 people and so it is not feasible to build a model using a CNN or any deep learning algorithm, unless we have sufficient data points. So, in these kinds of scenarios, we can resort to a sophisticated one-shot learning algorithm such as a siamese network, which can learn from fewer data points.

But how do siamese networks work? Siamese networks basically consist of two symmetrical neural networks both sharing the same weights and architecture and both joined together at the end using some energy function, **E**. The objective of our siamese network is to learn whether two input values are similar or dissimilar. Let's say we have two images, X_1 and **X2**, and we want to learn whether the two images are similar or dissimilar.

As shown in the following diagram, we feed the image X_1 to **Network A** and the image X_2 to another **Network B**. The role of both of these networks is to generate embeddings (feature vectors) for the input image. So, we can use any network that will give us embeddings. Since our input is an image, we can use a convolutional network for generating the embeddings, that is, for extracting features. Remember the role of the CNN here is only to extract features and not to classify. As we know that these networks should have the same weights and architecture, if our **Network A** is a three-layer CNN then our **Network B** should also be a three-layer CNN and we have to use the same set of weights for both of these networks. So, **Network A** and **Network B** will give us the embeddings for the input images X_1 and X_2 respectively. Then, we will feed these embeddings to the energy function, which tells us how similar the two inputs are. Energy functions are basically any similarity measure, such as Euclidean distance and cosine similarity.

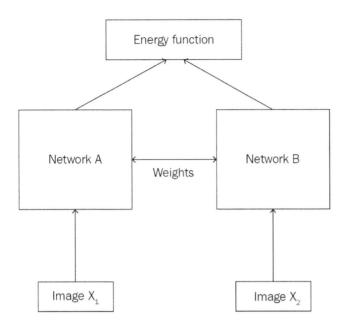

Siamese networks are not only used for face recognition, but they are also used extensively in applications where we don't have many data points and tasks where we need to learn similarity between two inputs. The applications of siamese networks include signature verification, similar question retrieval, object tracking, and more. We will study siamese networks in detail in the upcoming section.

Architecture of siamese networks

Now that we have a basic understanding of siamese networks, we will explore them in detail. The architecture of a siamese network is shown in the following diagram:

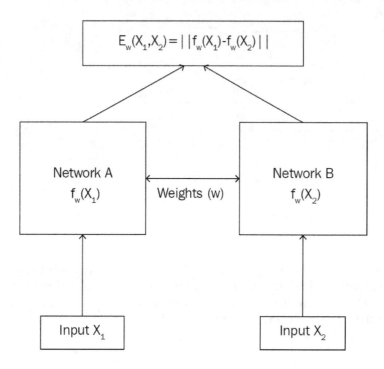

As you can see in the preceding diagram, a siamese network consists of two identical networks both sharing the same weights and architecture. Let's say we have two inputs, X_1 and X_2. We feed our input X_1 to **Network A**, that is, $\mathbf{f_w(X_1)}$, and we feed our input X_2 to **Network B**, that is, $\mathbf{f_w(X_2)}$. As you will notice, both of these networks have the same weights, $\mathbf{w}$, and they will generate embeddings for our input, X_1 and X_2. Then, we feed these embeddings to the energy function, $\mathbf{E}$, which will give us similarity between the two inputs.

It can be expressed as follows:

$$E_W(X_1, X_2) = ||f_W(X_1) - f_W(X_2)||$$

Let's say we use Euclidean distance as our energy function, then the value of $\mathbf{E}$ will be less, if X_1 and X_2 are similar. The value of $\mathbf{E}$ will be large if the input values are dissimilar.

Assume that you have two sentences, sentence 1 and sentence 2. We feed sentence 1 to **Network A** and sentence 2 to **Network B**. Let's say both our **Network A** and **Network B** are LSTM networks and they share the same weights. So, **Network A** and **Network B** will generate the word embeddings for sentence 1 and sentence 2 respectively. Then, we feed these embeddings to the energy function, which gives us the similarity score between the two sentences. But how can we train our siamese networks? How should the data be? What are the features and labels? What is our objective function?

The input to the siamese networks should be in pairs, **(X₁, X₂)**, along with their binary label, **Y ∈ (0, 1)**, stating whether the input pairs are a genuine pair (same) or an imposite pair (different). As you can see in the following table, we have sentences as pairs and the label implies whether the sentence pairs are genuine (1) or imposite (0):

Sentence pairs		Label
She is a beautiful girl	She is a gorgeous girl	1
Birds fly in the sky	What are you doing ?	0
I love Paris	I adore Paris	1
He just arrived	I am watching a movie	0

So, what is the loss function of our siamese network? Since the goal of the siamese network is not to perform a classification task but to understand the similarity between the two input values, we use the contrastive loss function.

It can be expressed as follows:

$$Contrastive\ Loss = Y(E)^2 + (1 - Y)max(margin - E, 0)^2$$

In the preceding equation, the value of **Y** is the true label, which will be **1** when the two input values are similar and **0** if the two input values are dissimilar, and **E** is our energy function, which can be any distance measure. The term **margin** is used to hold the constraint, that is, when two input values are dissimilar, and if their distance is greater than a margin, then they do not incur a loss.

Applications of siamese networks

As we understood, a siamese network learns by finding similarity between two input values using identical architecture. It is one of the most commonly used few-shot learning algorithms among tasks that involve computing similarity between two entities. It is powerful and robust and serves as a solution for a low data problem.

In the first paper in which siamese networks were published (https://papers.nips.cc/paper/769-signature-verification-using-a-siamese-time-delay-neural-network.pdf), the author depicts the significance of the network for the signature verification task. The objective of the signature verification task is to identify the authenticity of the signature. So, the author trained the siamese networks with genuine and imposite pairs of signatures and used a convolutional network for extracting features from the signature. After extracting features, they measured the distance between two feature vectors for identifying the similarity. So, when a new signature comes in, we extract the features and compare them with the stored feature vector of the signer. If the distance is less than a certain threshold, then we accept the signature as authentic, or else we reject the signature.

Siamese networks are also used extensively in NLP tasks. There is an interesting paper (http://www.aclweb.org/anthology/W16-1617) where the authors used a siamese network for computing text similarity. They used siamese networks as bidirectional units and used cosine similarity as an energy function for computing the similarity between texts.

The applications of siamese networks are endless; they've been stacked with various architectures for performing various tasks such as human action recognition, scene change detection, and machine translation.

Face recognition using siamese networks

We will understand the siamese network by building a face recognition model. The objective of our network is to understand whether two faces are similar or dissimilar. We use the AT&T Database of Faces, which can be downloaded from here: `https://www.cl.cam.ac.uk/research/dtg/attarchive/facedatabase.html`.

Once you have downloaded and extracted the archive, you can see the folders `s1`, `s2`, up to `s40`, as shown here:

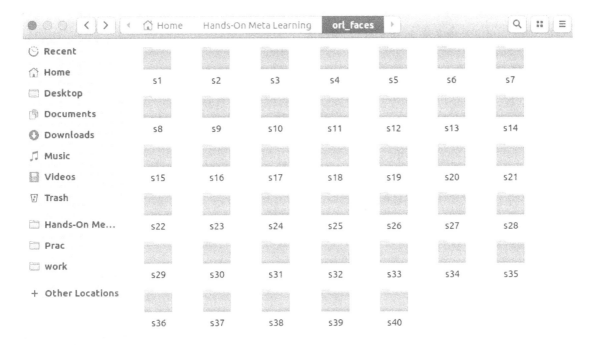

Each of these folders has 10 different images of a single person taken from various angles. For instance, let's open folder s1. As you can see, there are 10 different images of a single person:

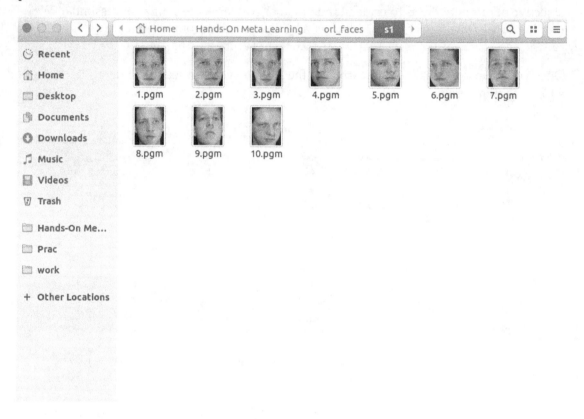

We open and check folder s13:

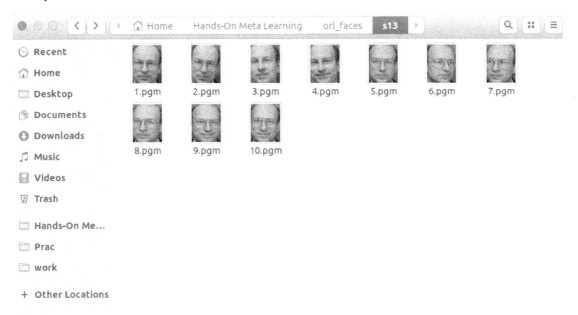

As we know that siamese networks require input values as a pair along with the label, we have to create our data in such a way. So, we will take two images randomly from the same folder and mark them as a genuine pair and we will take single images from two different folders and mark them as an imposite pair. A sample is shown in the following screenshot; as you can see, a genuine pair has images of the same person and the imposite pair has images of different people:

Input pair		Label
		Genuine
		Imposite
		Genuine
		Imposite

Once we have our data as pairs along with their labels, we train our siamese network. From the image pair, we feed one image to network A and another image to network B. The role of these two networks is only to extract the feature vectors. So, we use two convolution layers with **rectified linear unit** (**ReLU**) activations for extracting the features. Once we have learned the features, we feed the resultant feature vector from both of the networks to the energy function, which measures the similarity; we use Euclidean distance as our energy function. So, we train our network by feeding the image pair to learn the semantic similarity between them. Now, we will see this step by step. .

For better understanding, you can check the complete code, which is available as a Jupyter Notebook with an explanation here: `https://github.com/sudharsan13296/Hands-On-Meta-Learning-With-Python/blob/master/02.%20Face%20and%20Audio%20Recognition%20using%20Siamese%20Networks/2.4%20Face%20Recognition%20Using%20Siamese%20Network.ipynb`.

First, we will import the required libraries:

```
import re
import numpy as np
from PIL import Image

from sklearn.model_selection import train_test_split
from keras import backend as K
from keras.layers import Activation
from keras.layers import Input, Lambda, Dense, Dropout, Convolution2D,
MaxPooling2D, Flatten
from keras.models import Sequential, Model
from keras.optimizers import RMSprop
```

Now, we define a function for reading our input image. The `read_image` function takes as input an image and returns a NumPy array:

```
def read_image(filename, byteorder='>'):
    #first we read the image, as a raw file to the buffer
    with open(filename, 'rb') as f:
        buffer = f.read()
    #using regex, we extract the header, width, height and maxval of the
image
    header, width, height, maxval = re.search(
        b"(^P5\s(?:\s*#.*[\r\n])*"
        b"(\d+)\s(?:\s*#.*[\r\n])*"
        b"(\d+)\s(?:\s*#.*[\r\n])*"
        b"(\d+)\s(?:\s*#.*[\r\n]\s)*)", buffer).groups()
    #then we convert the image to numpy array using np.frombuffer which
interprets buffer as one dimensional array
    return np.frombuffer(buffer,
```

```
                                        dtype='u1' if int(maxval) < 256 else
     byteorder+'u2',

                                        count=int(width)*int(height),
                                        offset=len(header)
                                        ).reshape((int(height), int(width)))
```

For an example, let's open one image:

```
Image.open("data/orl_faces/s1/1.pgm")
```

When we feed this image to our `read_image` function, it will return as a NumPy array:

```
img = read_image('data/orl_faces/s1/1.pgm')
img.shape
(112, 92)
```

Now, we define another function, `get_data`, for generating our data. As we know, for the siamese network, data should be in the form of pairs (genuine and imposite) with a binary label.

First, we read the (`img1`, `img2`) images from the same directory and store them in the `x_genuine_pair` array and assign `y_genuine` to 1. Next, we read the (`img1`, `img2`) images from the different directory and store them in the `x_imposite` pair and assign `y_imposite` to 0.

Finally, we concatenate both `x_genuine_pair` and `x_imposite` to X and `y_genuine` and `y_imposite` to Y:

```
size = 2
total_sample_size = 10000


def get_data(size, total_sample_size):
    #read the image
    image = read_image('data/orl_faces/s' + str(1) + '/' + str(1) + '.pgm',
'rw+')
    #reduce the size
```

```
image = image[::size, ::size]
#get the new size
dim1 = image.shape[0]
dim2 = image.shape[1]

count = 0
#initialize the numpy array with the shape of [total_sample,
no_of_pairs, dim1, dim2]
x_geuine_pair = np.zeros([total_sample_size, 2, 1, dim1, dim2]) # 2 is
for pairs
y_genuine = np.zeros([total_sample_size, 1])
for i in range(40):
    for j in range(int(total_sample_size/40)):
        ind1 = 0
        ind2 = 0
        #read images from same directory (genuine pair)
        while ind1 == ind2:
            ind1 = np.random.randint(10)
            ind2 = np.random.randint(10)
        # read the two images
        img1 = read_image('data/orl_faces/s' + str(i+1) + '/' +
str(ind1 + 1) + '.pgm', 'rw+')
        img2 = read_image('data/orl_faces/s' + str(i+1) + '/' +
str(ind2 + 1) + '.pgm', 'rw+')
        #reduce the size
        img1 = img1[::size, ::size]
        img2 = img2[::size, ::size]
        #store the images to the initialized numpy array
        x_geuine_pair[count, 0, 0, :, :] = img1
        x_geuine_pair[count, 1, 0, :, :] = img2
        #as we are drawing images from the same directory we assign
label as 1. (genuine pair)
        y_genuine[count] = 1
        count += 1

count = 0
x_imposite_pair = np.zeros([total_sample_size, 2, 1, dim1, dim2])
y_imposite = np.zeros([total_sample_size, 1])
for i in range(int(total_sample_size/10)):
    for j in range(10):
        #read images from different directory (imposite pair)
        while True:
            ind1 = np.random.randint(40)
            ind2 = np.random.randint(40)
            if ind1 != ind2:
                break
        img1 = read_image('data/orl_faces/s' + str(ind1+1) + '/' +
str(j + 1) + '.pgm', 'rw+')
```

```
            img2 = read_image('data/orl_faces/s' + str(ind2+1) + '/' +
    str(j + 1) + '.pgm', 'rw+')

            img1 = img1[::size, ::size]
            img2 = img2[::size, ::size]

            x_imposite_pair[count, 0, 0, :, :] = img1
            x_imposite_pair[count, 1, 0, :, :] = img2
            #as we are drawing images from the different directory we
    assign label as 0. (imposite pair)
            y_imposite[count] = 0
            count += 1
    #now, concatenate, genuine pairs and imposite pair to get the whole
    data
    X = np.concatenate([x_geuine_pair, x_imposite_pair], axis=0)/255
    Y = np.concatenate([y_genuine, y_imposite], axis=0)

    return X, Y
```

Now, we generate our data and check our data size. As you can see, we have 20,000 data points and, out of these, 10,000 are genuine pairs and 10,000 are imposite pairs:

```
X, Y = get_data(size, total_sample_size)

X.shape
(20000, 2, 1, 56, 46)

Y.shape
(20000, 1)
```

Next, we split our data for training and testing with 75% training and 25% testing proportions:

```
x_train, x_test, y_train, y_test = train_test_split(X, Y, test_size=.25)
```

Now that we have successfully generated our data, we build our siamese network. First, we define the base network, which is basically a convolutional network used for feature extraction. We build two convolutional layers with ReLU activations and max pooling followed by a flat layer:

```
def build_base_network(input_shape):
    seq = Sequential()
    nb_filter = [6, 12]
    kernel_size = 3
    #convolutional layer 1
    seq.add(Convolution2D(nb_filter[0], kernel_size, kernel_size,
input_shape=input_shape,
                    border_mode='valid', dim_ordering='th'))
```

```
    seq.add(Activation('relu'))
    seq.add(MaxPooling2D(pool_size=(2, 2)))
    seq.add(Dropout(.25))
    #convolutional layer 2
    seq.add(Convolution2D(nb_filter[1], kernel_size, kernel_size,
border_mode='valid', dim_ordering='th'))
    seq.add(Activation('relu'))
    seq.add(MaxPooling2D(pool_size=(2, 2), dim_ordering='th'))
    seq.add(Dropout(.25))

    #flatten
    seq.add(Flatten())
    seq.add(Dense(128, activation='relu'))
    seq.add(Dropout(0.1))
    seq.add(Dense(50, activation='relu'))
    return seq
```

Next, we feed the image pair to the base network, which will return the embeddings, that is, feature vectors:

```
input_dim = x_train.shape[2:]
img_a = Input(shape=input_dim)
img_b = Input(shape=input_dim)

base_network = build_base_network(input_dim)
feat_vecs_a = base_network(img_a)
feat_vecs_b = base_network(img_b)
```

`feat_vecs_a` and `feat_vecs_b` are the feature vectors of our image pair. Next, we feed these feature vectors to the energy function to compute the distance between them, and we use Euclidean distance as our energy function:

```
def euclidean_distance(vects):
    x, y = vects
    return K.sqrt(K.sum(K.square(x - y), axis=1, keepdims=True))


def eucl_dist_output_shape(shapes):
    shape1, shape2 = shapes
    return (shape1[0], 1)

distance = Lambda(euclidean_distance,
output_shape=eucl_dist_output_shape)([feat_vecs_a, feat_vecs_b])
```

Now, we set the epoch length to 13, and we use the RMS prop for optimization and define our model:

```
epochs = 13
rms = RMSprop()

model = Model(input=[input_a, input_b], output=distance)
```

Next, we define our loss function as the `contrastive_loss` function and compile the model:

```
def contrastive_loss(y_true, y_pred):
    margin = 1
    return K.mean(y_true * K.square(y_pred) + (1 - y_true) *
K.square(K.maximum(margin - y_pred, 0)))

model.compile(loss=contrastive_loss, optimizer=rms)
```

Now, we train our model:

```
img_1 = x_train[:, 0]
img_2 = x_train[:, 1]

model.fit([img_1, img_2], y_train, validation_split=.25, batch_size=128,
verbose=2, nb_epoch=epochs)
```

You can see how the loss decreases over epochs:

```
Train on 11250 samples, validate on 3750 samples
Epoch 1/13
 - 60s - loss: 0.2179 - val_loss: 0.2156
Epoch 2/13
 - 53s - loss: 0.1520 - val_loss: 0.2102
Epoch 3/13
 - 53s - loss: 0.1190 - val_loss: 0.1545
Epoch 4/13
 - 55s - loss: 0.0959 - val_loss: 0.1705
Epoch 5/13
 - 52s - loss: 0.0801 - val_loss: 0.1181
Epoch 6/13
 - 52s - loss: 0.0684 - val_loss: 0.0821
Epoch 7/13
 - 52s - loss: 0.0591 - val_loss: 0.0762
Epoch 8/13
 - 52s - loss: 0.0526 - val_loss: 0.0655
Epoch 9/13
 - 52s - loss: 0.0475 - val_loss: 0.0662
Epoch 10/13
```

```
     - 52s - loss: 0.0444 - val_loss: 0.0469
 Epoch 11/13
     - 52s - loss: 0.0408 - val_loss: 0.0478
 Epoch 12/13
     - 52s - loss: 0.0381 - val_loss: 0.0498
 Epoch 13/13
     - 54s - loss: 0.0356 - val_loss: 0.0363
```

Now, we make predictions with test data:

```
pred = model.predict([x_test[:, 0], x_test[:, 1]])
```

Next, we define a function for computing accuracy:

```
def compute_accuracy(predictions, labels):
    return labels[predictions.ravel() < 0.5].mean()
```

Now, we the accuracy of model:

```
compute_accuracy(pred, y_test)
```

```
0.9779092702169625
```

Building an audio recognition model using siamese networks

In the last tutorial, we saw how to use siamese networks to recognize a face. Now we will see how to use siamese networks to recognize audio. We will train our network to differentiate between the sound of a dog and the sound of a cat. The dataset of cat and dog audio can be downloaded from here: `https://www.kaggle.com/mmoreaux/audio-cats-and-dogs#cats_dogs.zip`.

Once we have downloaded the data, we fragment our data into three folders: `Dogs`, `Sub_dogs`, and `Cats`. In `Dogs` and `Sub_dogs`, we place the dog's barking audio and in the `Cats` folder, we place the cat's audio. The objective of our network is to recognize whether the audio is a dog's barking or some different sound. As we know, for a siamese network, we need to feed input as a pair; we select an audio from the `Dogs` and `Sub_dogs` folders and mark them as a genuine pair and we select an audio from the `Dogs` and `Cats` folders and mark them as an imposite pair. That is, *(dogs, subdogs)* is a genuine pair and *(dogs, cats)* is an imposite pair.

Now, we will show, step-by-step, how to train our siamese network to recognize whether the audio is the dog's barking sound or a different sound.

For better understanding, you can check the complete code, which is available as a Jupyter Notebook with an explanation here: https://github.com/sudharsan13296/Hands-On-Meta-Learning-With-Python/blob/master/02.%20Face%20and%20Audio%20Recognition%20using%20Siamese%20Networks/2.5%20Audio%20Recognition%20using%20Siamese%20Network.ipynb.

First, we will load all of the necessary libraries:

```
#basic imports
import glob
import IPython
from random import randint

#data processing
import librosa
import numpy as np

#modelling
from sklearn.model_selection import train_test_split

from keras import backend as K
from keras.layers import Activation
from keras.layers import Input, Lambda, Dense, Dropout, Flatten
from keras.models import Model
from keras.optimizers import RMSprop
```

Before going ahead, we load and listen to the audio clips:

```
IPython.display.Audio("data/audio/Dogs/dog_barking_0.wav")

IPython.display.Audio("data/audio/Cats/cat_13.wav")
```

So, how can we feed this raw audio to our network? How can we extract meaningful features from the raw audio? As we know, neural networks accept only vectorized input, so we need to convert our audio into a feature vector. How can we do that? Well, there are several mechanisms through which we can generate embeddings for audio. One such popular mechanism is **Mel-Frequency Cepstral Coefficients** (**MFCC**). MFCC converts the short-term power spectrum of an audio using a linear cosine transform of a log power spectrum on a nonlinear mel scale of frequency. To learn more about MFCC, check out this nice tutorial: http://practicalcryptography.com/miscellaneous/machine-learning/guide-mel-frequency-cepstral-coefficients-mfccs/.

We will use the MFCC function from the `librosa` library for generating the audio embeddings. So, we define a function called `audio2vector`, which returns the audio embeddings given an audio file:

```
def audio2vector(file_path, max_pad_len=400):
    #read the audio file
    audio, sr = librosa.load(file_path, mono=True)

    #reduce the shape
    audio = audio[::3]
    #extract the audio embeddings using MFCC
    mfcc = librosa.feature.mfcc(audio, sr=sr)
    #as the audio embeddings length varies for different audio, we keep the
maximum length as 400
    #pad them with zeros

    pad_width = max_pad_len - mfcc.shape[1]
    mfcc = np.pad(mfcc, pad_width=((0, 0), (0, pad_width)),
mode='constant')

    return mfcc
```

We will load one audio file and see the embeddings:

```
audio_file = 'data/audio/Dogs/dog_barking_0.wav'
audio2vector(audio_file)
array([[-297.54905127, -288.37618855, -314.92037769, ...,       0.         ,
            0.         ,    0.        ],
       [  23.05969394,    9.55913148,   37.2173831 , ...,       0.         ,
            0.         ,    0.        ],
       [-122.06299523, -115.02627567, -108.18703056, ...,       0.         ,
            0.         ,    0.        ],

       ...,
       [  -6.40930836,   -2.8602708 ,   -2.12551478, ...,       0.         ,
            0.         ,    0.        ],
       [   0.70572914,    4.21777791,    4.62429301, ...,       0.         ,
            0.         ,    0.        ],
       [  -6.08997702,  -11.40687886,  -18.2415214 , ...,       0.         ,
            0.         ,    0.        ]])
```

Now that we have understood how to generate audio embeddings, we need to create the data for our siamese network. As we know, a siamese network accepts the data in a pair, so we define the function for getting our data. We will create the genuine pair as (Dogs, Sub_dogs) and assign the label as 1 and the imposite pair as (Dogs, Cats) and assign the label as 0:

```
def get_data():
    pairs = []
    labels = []
    Dogs = glob.glob('data/audio/Dogs/*.wav')
    Sub_dogs = glob.glob('data/audio/Sub_dogs/*.wav')
    Cats = glob.glob('data/audio/Cats/*.wav')
    np.random.shuffle(Sub_dogs)
    np.random.shuffle(Cats)
    for i in range(min(len(Cats),len(Sub_dogs))):
        #imposite pair
        if (i % 2) == 0:
pairs.append([audio2vector(Dogs[randint(0,3)]),audio2vector(Cats[i])])
            labels.append(0)
        #genuine pair
        else:
pairs.append([audio2vector(Dogs[randint(0,3)]),audio2vector(Sub_dogs[i])])
            labels.append(1)
    return np.array(pairs), np.array(labels)

X, Y = get_data("/home/sudarshan/sudarshan/Experiments/oneshot-
audio/data/")
```

Next, we split our data for training and testing with 75% training and 25% testing proportions:

```
X_train, X_test, y_train, y_test = train_test_split(X, Y, test_size=0.2)
```

Now that we have successfully generated our data, we build our siamese network. We define our base network, which is used for feature extraction, and we use three dense layers with a dropout layer in between:

```
def build_base_network(input_shape):
    input = Input(shape=input_shape)
    x = Flatten()(input)
    x = Dense(128, activation='relu')(x)
    x = Dropout(0.1)(x)
    x = Dense(128, activation='relu')(x)
    x = Dropout(0.1)(x)
    x = Dense(128, activation='relu')(x)
    return Model(input, x)
```

Next, we feed the audio pair to the base network, which will return the features:

```
input_dim = X_train.shape[2:]
audio_a = Input(shape=input_dim)
audio_b = Input(shape=input_dim)

base_network = build_base_network(input_dim)
feat_vecs_a = base_network(audio_a)
feat_vecs_b = base_network(audio_b)
```

`feat_vecs_a` and `feat_vecs_b` are the feature vectors of our audio pair. Next, we feed these feature vectors to the energy function to compute a distance between them, and we use Euclidean distance as our energy function:

```
def euclidean_distance(vects):
    x, y = vects
    return K.sqrt(K.sum(K.square(x - y), axis=1, keepdims=True))


def eucl_dist_output_shape(shapes):
    shape1, shape2 = shapes
    return (shape1[0], 1)

distance = Lambda(euclidean_distance,
    output_shape=eucl_dist_output_shape)([feat_vecs_a, feat_vecs_b])
```

Next, we set the epoch length to 13 and we use the RMS prop for optimization:

```
epochs = 13
rms = RMSprop()

model = Model(input=[audio_a, audio_b], output=distance)
```

Lastly, we define our loss function as `contrastive_loss` and compile the model:

```
def contrastive_loss(y_true, y_pred):
    margin = 1
    return K.mean(y_true * K.square(y_pred) + (1 - y_true) *
K.square(K.maximum(margin - y_pred, 0)))

model.compile(loss=contrastive_loss, optimizer=rms)
```

Now, we train our model:

```
audio1 = X_train[:, 0]
audio2 = X_train[:, 1]

model.fit([audio_1, audio_2], y_train, validation_split=.25,
          batch_size=128, verbose=2, nb_epoch=epochs)
```

You can how the loss over epochs:

```
Train on 8 samples, validate on 3 samples
Epoch 1/13
 - 0s - loss: 23594.8965 - val_loss: 1598.8439
Epoch 2/13
 - 0s - loss: 62360.9570 - val_loss: 816.7302
Epoch 3/13
 - 0s - loss: 17967.6230 - val_loss: 970.0378
Epoch 4/13
 - 0s - loss: 20030.3711 - val_loss: 358.9078
Epoch 5/13
 - 0s - loss: 11196.0547 - val_loss: 339.9991
Epoch 6/13
 - 0s - loss: 3837.2898 - val_loss: 381.9774
Epoch 7/13
 - 0s - loss: 2037.2965 - val_loss: 303.6652
Epoch 8/13
 - 0s - loss: 1434.4321 - val_loss: 229.1388
Epoch 9/13
 - 0s - loss: 2553.0562 - val_loss: 215.1207
Epoch 10/13
 - 0s - loss: 1046.6870 - val_loss: 197.1127
Epoch 11/13
 - 0s - loss: 569.4632 - val_loss: 183.8586
Epoch 12/13
 - 0s - loss: 759.0131 - val_loss: 162.3362
Epoch 13/13
 - 0s - loss: 819.8594 - val_loss: 120.3017
```

Summary

In this chapter, we have learned what siamese networks are and how to build face and audio recognition models using siamese networks. We explored the architecture of siamese networks, which basically consists of two identical neural networks both having the same weights and architecture and the output of these networks is plugged into some energy function to understand the similarity.

In the next chapter, we will learn about prototypical networks and the variants of the same, such as Gaussian prototypical and semi prototypical networks. We will also see how to use prototypical networks for omniglot character set classification.

Questions

1. What are siamese networks?
2. What is the contrastive loss function?
3. What is the energy function?
4. What is the desired data format for a siamese network?
5. What are the applications of siamese networks?

Further readings

- Siamese networks for object tracking: `https://arxiv.org/pdf/1606.09549.pdf`
- Siamese networks for image recognition: `https://www.cs.cmu.edu/~rsalakhu/papers/oneshot1.pdf`

Prototypical Networks and Their Variants

3

In the last chapter, we learned what siamese networks are and how they are used to perform few-shot learning tasks. We also explored how to use siamese networks for performing face and audio recognition. In this chapter, we will look at another interesting few-shot learning algorithm called a prototypical network, which has the ability to generalize even to the class that is not present in a training set. We will start off with understanding what prototypical networks are, after which we will see how to perform a classification task in an omniglot dataset using prototypical network. We will then see different variants of prototypical networks, such as Gaussian prototypical networks and semi-prototypical networks.

In this chapter, you will learn about the following:

- Prototypical networks
- The algorithm of prototypical networks
- Classification using prototypical networks
- Gaussian prototypical networks
- The Gaussian prototypical network algorithm
- Semi-prototypical network

Prototypical networks

Prototypical networks are yet another simple, efficient, few shot learning algorithm. Like siamese networks, a prototypical network tries to learn the metric space to perform classification. The basic idea of prototypical networks is to create a prototypical representation of each class and classify a query point (that is, a new point) based on the distance between the class prototype and the query point.

Let's say we have a support set comprising images of lions, elephants, and dogs, as shown in the following diagram:

Image (x$_i$)	Label (y$_i$)
	Lion
	Lion
	Elephant
	Elephant
	Dog
	Dog

Support set

So, we have three classes: *{lion, elephant, dog}*. Now we need to create a prototypical representation for each of these three class. How can we build the prototype of these three classes? First, we will learn the embeddings of each data point using an embedding function. The embedding function, $f_\phi()$, can be any function that can be used to extract features. Since our input is an image, we can use the convolutional network as our embedding function, which will extract features from the input image:

Image (x_i)	Label (y_i)		

Support set

Once we learn the embeddings of each data point, we take the mean embeddings of data points in each class and form the class prototype, as shown in the following diagram. So, a class prototype is basically the mean embeddings of data points in a class:

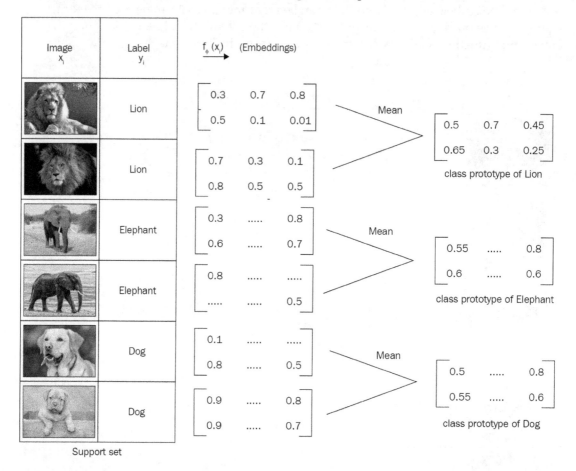

Support set

Similarly, when a new data point comes in, that is, a query point for which we want to predict the label, we will generate the embeddings for this new data point using the same embedding function that we used to create the class prototype—that is, we generate the embeddings for our query point using the convolutional network:

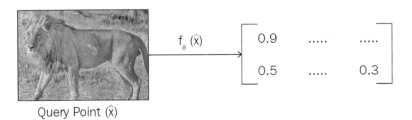

Query Point $(\hat{x})$

Once we have the embedding for our query point, we compare the distance between class prototype and query point embeddings to find which class the query point belongs to. We can use Euclidean distance as a measure for finding the distance between the class prototype and query points embeddings, as shown here:

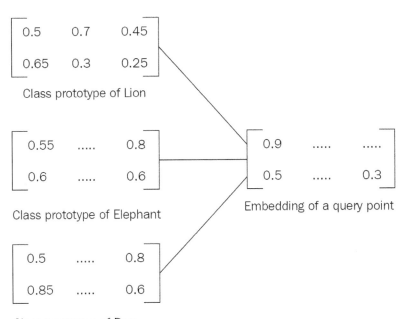

After finding the distance between the class prototype and query point embeddings, we apply softmax to this distance and get the probabilities. Since we have three classes, that is, lion, elephant and dog, we will get three probabilities. So, the class that has the highest probability will be the class of our query point.

Since we want our network to learn from a few data points, that is, we want to perform few-shot learning, we train our network in the same way. So, we use episodic training—for each episode, we randomly sample a few data points from each class in our dataset and we call that a support set and train the network using only the support set, instead of the whole dataset. Similarly, we randomly sample a point from the dataset as a query point and try to predict its class. So, in this way, our network is trained how to learn from a smaller set of data points.

The overall flow of our prototypical network is shown in the following diagram. As you can see, first, we will generate the embeddings for all of the data points in our support set and build the class prototype by taking the mean embeddings of data points in a class. We also generate the embeddings for our query point. Then, we compute the distance between class prototype and query point embeddings. We use Euclidean distance as a distance measure. Then, we apply softmax to this distance and get the probabilities. As you can see in the following diagram since our query point is a lion, the probability for lion is high—0.9:

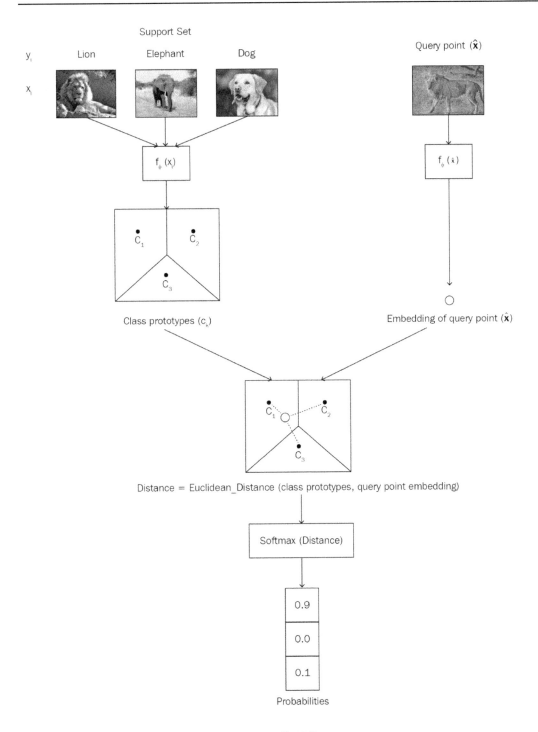

Prototypical networks are not only used for one-shot/few-shot learning but are also used in zero-shot learning. Consider the case where you have no data points per class, but you have the meta information containing a high-level description of each class. So, in those cases, we learn the embeddings from the meta information of each class to form the class prototype and then perform classification with the class prototype.

Algorithm

The algorithm of the prototypical networks is shown here:

1. Let's say we have the dataset, D, comprising $\{(x_1, y_1), (x_2, y_2), ... (x_n, y_n)\}$ where x is the feature and y is the class label.
2. Since we perform episodic training, we randomly sample n number of data points per each class from our dataset, D, and prepare our support set, S.
3. Similarly, we select n number of data points and prepare our query set, Q.
4. We learn the embeddings of the data points in our support set using our embedding function, $f_\varnothing ()$. The embedding function can be any feature extractor—say, a convolutional network for images and an LSTM network for text.
5. Once we have the embeddings for each data point, we compute the prototype of each class by taking the mean embeddings of the data points under each class:

$$i.\,e\; Class\; Prototype\,(c) = \frac{1}{S} \sum_{(x_i,y_i)\in s} f_\phi(x_i)$$

6. Similarly, we learn the query set embeddings.
7. We calculate the Euclidean distance, d, between query set embeddings and the class prototype.
8. We predict the probability, $p_\varnothing(y = k|x)$, of the class of a query set by applying softmax over the distance d:

$$i.\,e\; p_\phi(y = k|x) = \frac{exp(-d(f_\phi(x), c))}{\sum_k exp(-d(f_\phi(x), c))}$$

9. We compute the loss function, $J(\varnothing)$, as a negative log probability, $J(\varnothing) = -logp_\varnothing(y=k|x)$, and we try to minimize the loss using stochastic gradient descent.

Performing classification using prototypical networks

Now, we will see how to use prototypical networks to perform a classification task. We use an omniglot dataset for performing classification. This dataset comprises 1,623 handwritten characters from 50 different alphabets, and each character has 20 different examples written by different people. Since we want our network to learn from data, we train it in the same way. We sample five examples from each class and use that as our support set. We learn the embeddings of our support set using a sequence of four convolution blocks as our encoder and build the class prototype. Similarly, we sample five examples from each class for our query set, learn the query set embeddings, and predict the query set class by comparing the Euclidean distance between the query set embeddings and the class prototype. Let's better understand this by going through it step by step.

You can also check the code available as a Jupyter Notebook with an explanation here: https://github.com/sudharsan13296/Hands-On-Meta-Learning-With-Python/blob/master/03.%20Prototypical%20Networks%20and%20its%20Variants/3.3%20Omniglot%20Character%20set%20classification%20using%20Prototypical%20Network.ipynb.

First, we import all of the required libraries:

```
import os
import glob
from PIL import Image
import numpy as np
import tensorflow as tf
```

Now, we will explore and see what we got in our data. As we know, we have different characters from different alphabets and each character has twenty different variants written by different people. Let's plot and check some of them.

Let's plot one character from the Japanese alphabet:

```
Image.open('data/images/Japanese_(katakana)/character13/0608_01.png')
```

The same alphabet in a different variation:

```
Image.open('data/images/Japanese_(katakana)/character13/0608_13.png')
```

Let's see a character from the Sanskrit alphabet:

```
Image.open('data/images/Sanskrit/character13/0863_09.png')
```

```
Image.open('data/images/Sanskrit/character13/0863_13.png')
```

How can we convert this image into an array? We can use `np.array` to convert these images into an array and reshape it to 28 x 28:

```
image_name = 'data/images/Sanskrit/character13/0863_13.png'
alphabet, character, rotation = 'Sanskrit/character13/rot000'.split('/')
rotation = float(rotation[3:])
```

You can see the output as follows:

```
array([[1., 1., 1., 1., 1., 1., 1., 1., 1., 1., 1., 1., 1., 1., 1., 1., 1.,
1., 1., 1., 1., 1., 1., 1., 1., 1., 1.], [1., 1., 1., 1., 1., 1., 1.,
1., 1., 1., 1., 1., 1., 1., 1., 0., 1., 1., 1., 1., 1., 1., 0., 1., 1., 1.,
0., 1.], [1., 1., 1., 1., 1., 1., 1., 1., 1., 1., 1., 1., 1., 1., 1., 1.,
1., 1., 1., 1., 1., 1., 1., 1., 1., 1., 1.], [1., 1., 1., 1., 1., 1.,
1., 1., 1., 1., 1., 1., 1., 1., 1., 1., 1., 1., 1., 1., 1., 1., 1., 1., 1.,
1., 1., 1.]], dtype=float32)
```

Now that we have understood what is in our dataset, we load our dataset:

```
root_dir = 'data/'
```

We have the splitting details in the /data/omniglot/splits/train.txt file which has the language name, character number, and rotation information and images in /data/omniglot/data/:

```
train_split_path = os.path.join(root_dir, 'splits', 'train.txt')

with open(train_split_path, 'r') as train_split:
    train_classes = [line.rstrip() for line in train_split.readlines()]
```

We find the number of classes as follows:

```
#number of classes
no_of_classes = len(train_classes)
```

Now, we set number of examples to 20, as we have 20 examples per class in our dataset, and we set the image width and height to 28 x 28:

```
#number of examples
num_examples = 20

#image width
img_width = 28

#image height
img_height = 28
channels = 1
```

Next, we initialize our training dataset with a shape as a number of classes, number of examples, and image height and width:

```
train_dataset = np.zeros([no_of_classes, num_examples, img_height,
img_width], dtype=np.float32)
```

Now, we read all of the images, convert them into a NumPy array and store it in our train_dataset array with their label and values, that is, train_dataset = [label, values]:

```
for label, name in enumerate(train_classes):
    alphabet, character, rotation = name.split('/')
    rotation = float(rotation[3:])
    img_dir = os.path.join(root_dir, 'data', alphabet, character)
    img_files = sorted(glob.glob(os.path.join(img_dir, '*.png')))
    for index, img_file in enumerate(img_files):
        values = 1. -
np.array(Image.open(img_file).rotate(rotation).resize((img_width,
img_height)), np.float32, copy=False)
        train_dataset[label, index] = values
```

The shape of the training data would be as follows:

```
train_dataset.shape

(4112, 20, 28, 28)
```

Now that we have loaded our training data, we need to create embeddings for them. We generate the embeddings using convolution operation as our input values are images. So, we define a convolutional block with 64 filters with batch normalization and ReLU as the activation function. We follow this with performing a max pooling operation:

```
def convolution_block(inputs, out_channels, name='conv'):

    conv = tf.layers.conv2d(inputs, out_channels, kernel_size=3,
padding='SAME')
    conv = tf.contrib.layers.batch_norm(conv, updates_collections=None,
decay=0.99, scale=True, center=True)
    conv = tf.nn.relu(conv)
    conv = tf.contrib.layers.max_pool2d(conv, 2)
    return conv
```

Now, we define our embedding function, which gives us the embedding comprising four convolutional blocks:

```
def get_embeddings(support_set, h_dim, z_dim, reuse=False):

        net = convolution_block(support_set, h_dim)
        net = convolution_block(net, h_dim)
        net = convolution_block(net, h_dim)
        net = convolution_block(net, z_dim)
        net = tf.contrib.layers.flatten(net)
        return net
```

 Remember, we don't use our whole dataset for training; since we are using one-shot learning, we sample some data points from each class as a support set and train the network using the support set in an episodic fashion.

Now, we define some of the important variables—we consider a 50-way five-shot learning scenario:

```
#number of classes
num_way = 50

#number of examples per class in a support set
num_shot = 5
```

```
#number of query points for query set
num_query = 5

#number of examples
num_examples = 20

h_dim = 64
z_dim = 64
```

Next, we initialize placeholders for our support and query sets:

```
support_set = tf.placeholder(tf.float32, [None, None, img_height,
img_width, channels])
query_set = tf.placeholder(tf.float32, [None, None, img_height, img_width,
channels])
```

And we store the shape of our support and query sets in `support_set_shape` and `query_set_shape` respectively:

```
support_set_shape = tf.shape(support_set)
query_set_shape = tf.shape(query_set)
```

We get the number of classes, the number of data points in the support set, and the number of data points in the query set for initializing our support and query sets:

```
num_classes, num_support_points = support_set_shape[0],
support_set_shape[1]
num_query_points = query_set_shape[1]
```

Next, we define the placeholder for our label:

```
y = tf.placeholder(tf.int64, [None, None])

#convert the label to one hot
y_one_hot = tf.one_hot(y, depth=num_classes)
```

Now, we generate the embeddings for our support set using our embedding function:

```
support_set_embeddings = get_embeddings(tf.reshape(support_set,
[num_classes * num_support_points, img_height, img_width, channels]),
h_dim, z_dim)
```

We compute the prototype of each class, which is the mean vector of the support set embeddings of the class:

```
embedding_dimension = tf.shape(support_set_embeddings)[-1]

class_prototype = tf.reduce_mean(tf.reshape(support_set_embeddings,
[num_classes, num_support_points, embedding_dimension]), axis=1)
```

Next, we use our same embedding function to get embeddings of the query set:

```
query_set_embeddings = get_embeddings(tf.reshape(query_set, [num_classes *
num_query_points, img_height, img_width, channels]), h_dim, z_dim,
reuse=True)
```

Now that we have the class prototype and query set embeddings, we define a distance function that gives us the distance between the class prototypes and query set embeddings:

```
def euclidean_distance(a, b):

    N, D = tf.shape(a)[0], tf.shape(a)[1]
    M = tf.shape(b)[0]
    a = tf.tile(tf.expand_dims(a, axis=1), (1, M, 1))
    b = tf.tile(tf.expand_dims(b, axis=0), (N, 1, 1))
    return tf.reduce_mean(tf.square(a - b), axis=2)
```

We calculate the distance between the class prototype and query set embeddings:

```
distance = euclidean_distance(class_prototype,query_set_embeddings)
```

Next, we get the probability for each class as a softmax to the distance:

```
predicted_probability = tf.reshape(tf.nn.log_softmax(-distance),
[num_classes, num_query_points, -1])
```

Then, we compute the loss:

```
loss = -tf.reduce_mean(tf.reshape(tf.reduce_sum(tf.multiply(y_one_hot,
predicted_probability), axis=-1), [-1]))
```

We calculate the accuracy as follows:

```
accuracy =
tf.reduce_mean(tf.to_float(tf.equal(tf.argmax(predicted_probability,
axis=-1), y)))
```

Then, we use the Adam optimizer for minimizing the loss:

```
train = tf.train.AdamOptimizer().minimize(loss)
```

Now, we start our TensorFlow session and train the model:

```
sess = tf.InteractiveSession()
init = tf.global_variables_initializer()
sess.run(init)
```

We define the number of epochs and the number of episodes:

```
num_epochs = 20
num_episodes = 100
```

Next, we start the episodic training—that is, for each episode, we sample data points, build the support and query sets, and train the model:

```
for epoch in range(num_epochs):
    for episode in range(num_episodes):
        # select 60 classes
        episodic_classes = np.random.permutation(no_of_classes)[:num_way]
        support = np.zeros([num_way, num_shot, img_height, img_width],
dtype=np.float32)
        query = np.zeros([num_way, num_query, img_height, img_width],
dtype=np.float32)
        for index, class_ in enumerate(episodic_classes):
            selected = np.random.permutation(num_examples)[:num_shot +
num_query]
            support[index] = train_dataset[class_, selected[:num_shot]]
            # 5 querypoints per classs
            query[index] = train_dataset[class_, selected[num_shot:]]
        support = np.expand_dims(support, axis=-1)
        query = np.expand_dims(query, axis=-1)
        labels = np.tile(np.arange(num_way)[:, np.newaxis], (1,
num_query)).astype(np.uint8)
        _, loss_, accuracy_ = sess.run([train, loss, accuracy],
feed_dict={support_set: support, query_set: query, y:labels})
        if (episode+1) % 20 == 0:
            print('Epoch {} : Episode {} : Loss: {}, Accuracy:
{}'.format(epoch+1, episode+1, loss_, accuracy_))
```

Gaussian prototypical network

Now, we will look at a variant of a prototypical network, called a Gaussian prototypical network. We just learned how a prototypical network learns the embeddings of the data points and how it builds the class prototype by taking the mean embeddings of each class and uses the class prototype for performing classification.

In a Gaussian prototypical network, along with generating embeddings for the data points, we add a confidence region around them, characterized by a Gaussian covariance matrix. Having a confidence region helps in characterizing the quality of individual data points and would be useful in the case of noisy and less homogeneous data.

So, in Gaussian prototypical networks, the output of the encoder will be embeddings, as well as the covariance matrix. Instead of using the full covariance matrix, we either include a radius or diagonal component from the covariance matrix along with the embeddings:

- **Radius component:** If we use the radius component of the covariance matrix, then the dimension of our covariance matrix would be 1, as the radius is just a single number.
- **Diagonal component:** If we use the diagonal component of the covariance matrix, then the dimension of our covariance matrix would be the same as the embedding matrix dimension.

Also, instead of using the covariance matrix directly, we use the inverse of a covariance matrix. We can convert the raw covariance matrix into the inverse covariance matrix using any of the following methods. Let S_{raw} be the covariance matrix and S be the inverse covariance matrix:

- $S = 1 + Softplus(S_{raw})$
- $S = 1 + sigmoid(S_{raw})$
- $S = 1 + 4 * sigmoid(S_{raw})$
- $S = offset + scale * softplus(S_{raw}/div)$, where *offset* and *scale* are trainable parameters

So, the encoder, along with generating embedding for the input, also returns the covariance matrix. We use either the diagonal or radius components of the covariance matrix. Also, instead of using a covariance matrix directly, we use the inverse covariance matrix.

But what is the use of having the covariance matrix along with the embeddings? As said earlier, it adds the confidence region around the data points and is very useful in the case of noisy data. Look at the following diagram. Let's say we have two classes, **A** and **B**. The dark dots represent the embeddings of the data point, and the circles around the dark dots indicate the covariance matrices. A big dotted circle represents the overall covariance matrix for a class. A star in the middle indicates the class prototype. As you can see, having this covariance matrix around the embeddings gives us a confidence region around the data point and for class prototypes:

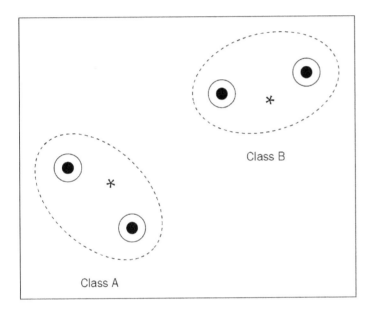

Let's better understand this by looking at the code. Let's say we have an image, X, and we want to generate embeddings for the image. Let's represent the covariance matrix by sigma. First, we select what component of the covariance matrix we want to use—that is, whether we want to use the diagonal or radius component. If we use the radius component, then our covariance matrix dimension would be just one. If we opt for the diagonal component, then the size of the covariance matrix would be same as the embedding dimension:

```
if component =='radius':
    covariance_matrix_dim = 1
else:
    covariance_matrix_dim = embedding_dim
```

Now, we define our encoder. Since our input is an image, we use a convolutional block as our encoder. So, we define the size of filters, a number of filters, and the pooling layer size:

```
filters = [3,3,3,3]
num_filters = [64,64,64,embedding_dim +covariance_matrix_dim]
pools = [2,2,2,2]
```

We initialize embeddings as our image, X:

```
previous_channels = 1
embeddings = X
weight = []
bias = []
conv_relu = []
conv = []
conv_pooled = []
```

Then, we perform the convolutional operation and get the embeddings:

```
for i in range(len(filters)):

    filter_size = filters[i]
    num_filter = num_filters[i]
    pool = pools[i]
    weight.append(tf.get_variable("weights_"+str(i), shape=[filter_size,
filter_size, previous_channels, num_filter])
    bias.append(tf.get_variable("bias_"+str(i), shape=[num_filter]))
    conv.append(tf.nn.conv2d(embeddings, weight[i], strides=[1,1,1,1],
padding='SAME') + bias[i])
    conv_relu.append(tf.nn.relu(conv[i]))
    conv_pooled.append(tf.nn.max_pool(conv_relu[i], ksize =
[1,pool,pool,1], strides=[1,pool,pool,1], padding = "VALID"))

    previous_channels = num_filter
    embeddings = conv_pooled[i]
```

We take the output of the last convolutional layer as our embeddings and reshape the result to have embeddings, as well as the covariance matrix:

```
X_encoded = tf.reshape(embeddings, [-1,embedding_dim + covariance_matrix_dim
])
```

Now, we split the embeddings and raw covariance matrix, as we need to convert the raw covariance matrix into the inverse covariance matrix:

```
embeddings, raw_covariance_matrix = tf.split(X_encoded, [embedding_dim,
covariance_matrix_dim], 1)
```

Next, we calculate the inverse of a covariance matrix using any of the discussed methods:

```
if inverse_transform_type == "softplus":
    offset = 1.0
    scale = 1.0
    inv_covariance_matrix = offset + scale *
tf.nn.softplus(raw_covariance_matrix)


elif inverse_transform_type == "sigmoid":
    offset = 1.0
    scale = 1.0
    inv_covariance_matrix = offset + scale *
tf.sigmoid(raw_covariance_matrix)


elif inverse_transform_type == "sigmoid_2":
    offset = 1.0
    scale = 4.0
    inv_covariance_matrix = offset + scale *
tf.sigmoid(raw_covariance_matrix)

elif inverse_transform_type == "other":

    init = tf.constant(1.0)
    scale = tf.get_variable("scale", initializer=init)
    div = tf.get_variable("div", initializer=init)
    offset = tf.get_variable("offset", initializer=init)

    inv_covariance_matrix = offset + scale *
tf.nn.softplus(raw_covariance_matrix/div)
```

So far, we have seen that we calculate the covariance matrix along with embeddings of an input. What's next? How can we compute the class prototype? The class prototype, $\vec{p_c}$, can be computed as follows:

$$\vec{p_c} = \frac{\sum_i s_i^c \cdot x_i^c}{\sum_i s_i^c}$$

In this equation, s_i^c is the diagonal of the inverse covariance matrix, x_i^c denotes the embeddings and superscript c denotes the class.

After computing the prototype for each of the classes, we learn the embedding of the query point. Let $\vec{x'}$ be the embedding of a query point. Then, we compute the distance between the query point embedding and class prototype as follows:

$$distance = \sqrt{(\vec{x'} - \vec{p_c})^T \vec{s_i^c} . (\vec{x'} - \vec{p_c})}$$

Finally, we predict the class of a query set ($\hat{y}$), which has the minimum distance with the class prototype:

$$\hat{y} = argmin_c(distance)$$

Algorithm

Now, we will better understand the Gaussian prototypical network by going through it step by step:

1. Let's say we have a dataset, $D = \{(x_1, y_1), (x_2, y_2), ... (x_i, y_i)\}$, where x is the feature and y is the label. Let's say we have a binary label, which means we have only two classes, 0 and 1. We will sample data points at random without replacement from each of the classes from our dataset, D, and create our support set, S.
2. Similarly, we sample data points at random per class and create the query set, Q.
3. We will pass the support set to our embedding function, $f()$. The embedding function will generate the embeddings for our support set, along with the covariance matrix.
4. We calculate the inverse of the covariance matrix.
5. We compute the prototype of each class in the support set as follows:

$$Prototype(\vec{p}^c) = \frac{\sum_i \vec{s_i^c} . \vec{x_i^c}}{\sum_i \vec{s_i^c}}$$

In this equation, s_i^c is the diagonal of the inverse covariance matrix, x_i^c denotes the embeddings of the support set and superscript c denotes the class.

6. After computing the prototype of each class in the support set, we learn the embeddings for the query set, Q. Let's say x' is the embedding of the query point.
7. We calculate the distance of the query point embeddings to the class prototypes as follows:

$$distance = \sqrt{(\vec{x'} - \vec{p_c})^T \vec{s_i^c} \cdot (\vec{x'} - \vec{p_c})}$$

8. After calculating the distance between the class prototype and query set embeddings, we predict the class of the query set as a class that has a minimum distance, as follows:

$$\hat{y} = argmin_c(distance)$$

Semi-prototypical networks

Now, we will see another interesting variant of prototypical networks called the semi-prototypical network. It deals with handling unlabeled examples. As we know, in the prototypical network, we compute the prototype of each class by taking the mean embedding of each class and then predict the class of query set by finding the distance between query points to the class prototypes.

Consider the case where our dataset contains some of the unlabeled data points: how do we compute the class prototypes of these unlabeled data points?

Let's say we have a support set, $S = (x_1, y_1), (x_2, y_2). \ldots . (x_k, y_k)$ where x is the feature and y is the label, and a query set, $Q = (x'_1, y'_1), (x'_2, y'_2). \ldots . (x'_k, y'_k)$. Along with these, we have one more set called the unlabeled set, R, where we have only unlabeled examples, $R = \{\tilde{x}_1, \tilde{x}_2. \ldots . \tilde{x}_k\}$.

So, what can we do with this unlabeled set?

First, we will compute the class prototype with all the examples given in the support set. Next, we use soft k-means and assign the class for unlabeled examples in R—that is, we assign the class for unlabeled examples in R *by* calculating the Euclidean distance between class prototypes and unlabelled example.

However, the problem with this approach is that, since we are using soft k-means, all of the unlabeled examples will belong to any of the class prototypes. Let us say, we have three classes in the support set, *{lion, elephant, dog}*; if our unlabeled example has a data point representing a cat, then it is not meaningful to place the cat in any of the class in the support set. So, instead of adding the data point to the existing class, we assign a new class for the unlabeled examples, called the distractor class.

But even with this approach, we will run into another problem because the distractor class itself will have high variance. For example, consider our unlabeled set, R, contains completely unrelated data points such as *{cats, helicopter, bus, and others}*; in this case, it is not suggested to keep all of the unlabeled examples in a single class called the distractor class, as they are already impure and unrelated to each other.

So, we remodel the distractor class as examples that are not within some threshold distance of all of the class prototypes. How can we compute this threshold? First, we compute the normalized distance between unlabeled examples in the unlabeled set R to all of the class prototypes. Next, we compute the threshold for each class prototype by feeding various statistics of the normalized distance, such as min, max, skewness, and kurtosis, to a neural network. Based on this threshold, we add or ignore the unlabeled examples to the class prototypes.

Summary

In this chapter, we started off with prototypical networks, and we saw how a prototypical network computes the class prototype using the embedding function and predicts the class label of the query set by comparing the Euclidean distance between the class prototype and query set embeddings. Following this, we experimented with a prototypical network by performing classification on an omniglot dataset. Then, we learned about the Gaussian prototypical network, which, along with the embeddings, also uses the covariance matrix to compute the class prototype. Following this, we explored semi-prototypical networks, which are used to handle semi-supervised classes. In the next chapter, we will learn about relation and matching networks.

Questions

1. What is a prototypical network?
2. What is the use of computing embeddings?
3. How do we calculate the class prototype?
4. What is a Gaussian prototypical network?
5. How do Gaussian prototypical networks differ from vanilla ones?
6. What are the different components of the covariance matrix used in a Gaussian prototypical network?

Further reading

- Prototypical networks: https://arxiv.org/pdf/1703.05175.pdf
- Gaussian prototypical networks: https://arxiv.org/pdf/1708.02735.pdf
- Semi-prototypical networks: https://arxiv.org/pdf/1803.00676.pdf

Relation and Matching Networks Using TensorFlow

4

In the last chapter, we learned about prototypical networks and how variants of prototypical networks, such as Gaussian prototypical and semi-prototypical networks, are used for one-shot learning. We have seen how prototypical networks make use of embeddings to perform classification tasks.

In this chapter, we will learn about relation networks and matching networks. First, we will see what a relation network is and how it is used in one-shot, few-shot, and zero-shot learning settings, after which we will learn how to build a relation network using TensorFlow. Later in this chapter, we will learn about matching networks and how they are used in few-shot learning. We will also see different types of embedding functions used in matching networks. At the end of this chapter, we will see how to build matching networks in Tensorflow.

In this chapter, we will learn about the following:

- Relation networks
- Relation networks in one-shot, few-shot, and zero-shot settings
- Building relation networks using TensorFlow
- Matching networks
- The embedding functions of a matching network
- The architecture of matching networks
- Matching networks in TensorFlow

Relation networks

Now, we will see another interesting one-shot learning algorithm, called a relation network. It is one of the simplest and most efficient one-shot learning algorithms. We will explore how relation networks are used in one-shot, few-shot, and zero-shot learning settings.

Relation networks in one-shot learning

A relation network consists of two important functions: the embedding function, denoted by f_φ, and the relation function, denoted by g_ϕ. The embedding function is used for extracting the features from the input. If our input is an image, then we can use a convolutional network as our embedding function, which will give us the feature vectors/embeddings of an image. If our input is a text, then we can use LSTM networks to get the embeddings of the text.

As we know, in one-shot learning, we have only a single example per class. For example, let's say our support set contains three classes with one example per class. As shown in the following diagram, we have a support set containing three classes, *{lion, elephant, dog}*:

Image (x$_i$)	Label (y$_i$)
	Lion
	Elephant
	Dog

Support Set

And let's say we have a query image, x_j, as shown in the following diagram, and we want to predict the class of this query image:

Query image (x_j)

First, we take each image, x_i, from the support set and pass it to the embedding function, $f_\varphi(x_i)$, for extracting the features. Since our support set has images, we can use a convolution network as our embedding function for learning the embeddings. The embedding function will give us the feature vector of each of the data points in the support set. Similarly, we will learn the embeddings of our query image, x_j, by passing it to the embedding function, $f_\varphi(x_j)$.

So, once we have the feature vectors of the support set, $f_\varphi(x_i)$, and query set, $f_\varphi(x_j)$, we combine them using an operator, Z. Here Z can be any combination operator; we use concatenation as an operator for combining the feature vectors of support and query set—that is, $Z(f_\varphi(x_i), f_\varphi(x_j))$.

As shown in the following figure, we will combine the feature vectors of the support set, $f_\varphi(x_i)$, and query set, $f_\varphi(x_j)$. But what is the use of combining like this? It will help us to understand how the feature vector of an image in the support set is related to the feature vector of a query image. In our example, it will help us to understand how the feature vectors of images of a lion, an elephant and a dog are related to the feature vector of the query image:

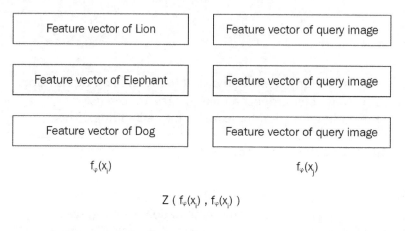

Feature vector of Lion	Feature vector of query image
Feature vector of Elephant	Feature vector of query image
Feature vector of Dog	Feature vector of query image

$$f_\varphi(x_i) \qquad\qquad f_\varphi(x_j)$$

$$Z\ (\ f_\varphi(x_i)\ ,\ f_\varphi(x_j)\ )$$

Feature concatenation

But how can we measure this relatedness? This is why we use a relation function, g_ϕ. We pass these combined feature vectors to the relation function, which will generate the relation score ranging from 0 to 1, representing the similarity between samples in the support set, x_i, and samples in the query set, x_j.

The following equation shows how we compute the relation score in a relation network:

$$r_{ij} = g_\phi(Z(f_\varphi(x_i), f_\varphi(x_j)))$$

In this equation, r_{ij} denotes the relation score representing similarity between each of the classes in the support set and the query image. Since we have three classes in the support set and one image in the query set, we will have three scores indicating how all three classes in the support set are similar to the query image.

The overall representation of a relation network in a one-shot learning setting is shown in the following diagram:

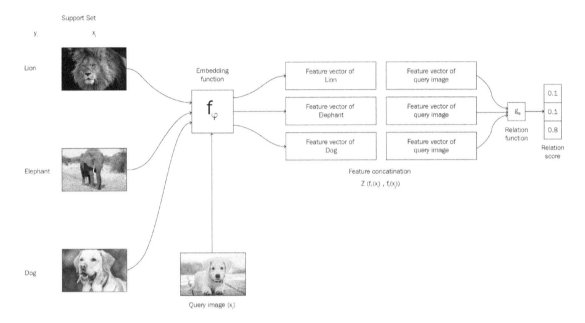

Relation networks in few-shot learning

We have seen how we take a single image belonging to each of the classes in the support set and compare their relation to the image in the query set in the one-shot learning setting of our relation network. But in a few-shot learning setting, we will have more than one data point per class. How do we learn the feature representation here using our embedding function?

Say we have a support set containing more than one image for each of the classes, as shown in the following diagram:

In this case, we will learn the embedding of each point in the support set and perform element-wise addition of embeddings of all of the data points belonging to each class. So, we will have embeddings for each of the classes, which is the element-wise summed embeddings of all of the data points in that class:

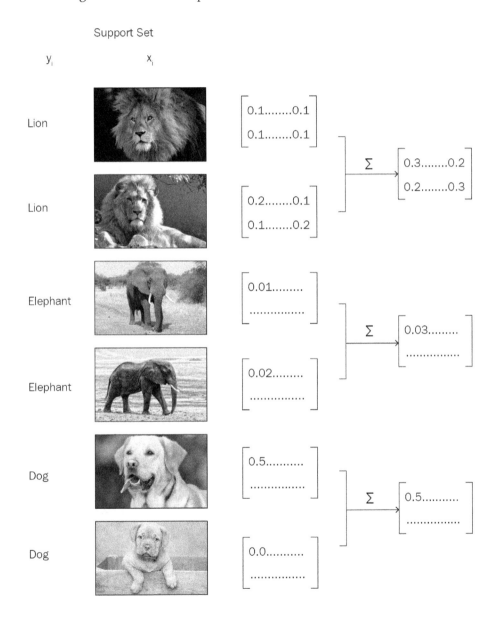

We can extract the feature vector of our query image using the embedding function as usual. Next, we combine the feature vectors of the support and query sets using the concatenation operator, Z. We perform concatenation, then we feed our concatenated feature vectors to the relation function and get the relation scores, which represent the similarity between each of the classes in the support set and the query set.

The overall representation of a relation network in a few-shot learning setting is shown in the following figure:

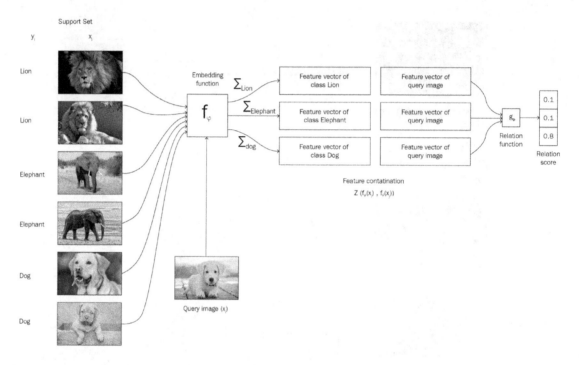

Relation networks in zero-shot learning

Now that we have understood how to use a relation network in one-shot and few-shot learning tasks, we will see how to use relation networks in a zero-shot learning setting where we will not have any data points under each class. However in zero-shot learning, we will have meta information which is information about the attributes of each class and that will be encoded into the semantic vector, v_c, where the subscript c represents the class.

Instead of using a single embedding function for learning the embeddings of support and query sets, we use two different embedding functions, $f_{\varphi 1}$ and $f_{\varphi 2}$ respectively. First, we will learn the embeddings of the semantic vector, v_c, using $f_{\varphi 1}$ and learn the embeddings of the query set, x_j, using $f_{\varphi 2}$. Now we will concatenate these embeddings using our concatenation operation, Z:

$$Z(f_{\varphi 1}(v_c), f_{\varphi 2}(x_j))$$

Then, we will feed this result to the relation function and compute the relation score as follows:

$$r_{ij} = g_\phi(Z(f_{\varphi 1}(v_c), f_{\varphi 2}(x_j)))$$

Loss function

What would be the loss function of the relation network? We will use the **Mean Squared Error** (**MSE**) as a loss function. Although it is a classification problem and MSE is not a standard measure for classification problems, the author of the relation network depicts that, since we are predicting relation scores, it can be considered a regression problem; despite that, for ground truths, we can only automatically generate {0, 1} targets.

So, our loss function can be represented as follows:

$$\varphi, \phi < -argmin_{\phi,\varphi} \sum_{i=1}^{m} \sum_{j=1}^{n} (r_{i,j} - 1(y_i == y_j))^2$$

Where φ, ϕ are the parameters of our embedding function, f, and relation function, g respectively.

Building relation networks using TensorFlow

The relation function is pretty simple, right? We will understand relation networks better by implementing one in TensorFlow.

You can also check the code available as a Jupyter Notebook with an explanation here:
`https://github.com/sudharsan13296/Hands-On-Meta-Learning-With-Python/blob/`
`master/04.%20Relation%20and%20Matching%20Networks%20Using%20Tensorflow/4.`
`5%20Building%20Relation%20Network%20Using%20Tensorflow.ipynb`.

First, we import all of the required libraries:

```
import tensorflow as tf
import numpy as np
```

We will randomly generate our data points. Let's say we have two classes in our dataset; we will randomly generate some 1,000 data points for each of these classes:

```
classA = np.random.rand(1000,18)
ClassB = np.random.rand(1000,18)
```

We create our dataset by combining both of these classes:

```
data = np.vstack([classA, ClassB])
```

Now, we set the labels; we assign the 1 label for `classA` and the 0 label for `classB`:

```
label = np.vstack([np.ones((len(classA),1)),np.zeros((len(ClassB),1))])
```

So, our dataset will have 2,000 records:

```
data.shape
(2000, 18)
```

Now, we will define the placeholders for our support and query sets:

```
xi = tf.placeholder(tf.float32, [None, 9])
xj = tf.placeholder(tf.float32, [None, 9])
```

Define the placeholder for the y label, as follows:

```
y = tf.placeholder(tf.float32, [None, 1])
```

Now, we will define our embedding function that will learn the embeddings of the support and query sets. We will use a normal feedforward network as our embedding function:

```
def embedding_function(x):
    weights = tf.Variable(tf.truncated_normal([9,1]))
    bias = tf.Variable(tf.truncated_normal([1]))
    a = (tf.nn.xw_plus_b(x,weights,bias))
    embeddings = tf.nn.relu(a)
    return embeddings
```

We compute the embeddings for the support set:

```
f_xi = embedding_function(xi)
```

We compute the embeddings for the query set:

```
f_xj = embedding_function(xj)
```

Now that we have calculated the embeddings and have the feature vectors, we combine both the support set and query set feature vectors:

```
Z = tf.concat([f_xi,f_xj],axis=1)
```

We define our relation function as three-layered neural network with ReLU activations:

```
def relation_function(x):
    w1 = tf.Variable(tf.truncated_normal([2,3]))
    b1 = tf.Variable(tf.truncated_normal([3]))
    w2 = tf.Variable(tf.truncated_normal([3,5]))
    b2 = tf.Variable(tf.truncated_normal([5]))
    w3 = tf.Variable(tf.truncated_normal([5,1]))
    b3 = tf.Variable(tf.truncated_normal([1]))
    #layer1
    z1 = (tf.nn.xw_plus_b(x,w1,b1))
    a1 = tf.nn.relu(z1)
    #layer2
    z2 = tf.nn.xw_plus_b(a1,w2,b2)
    a2 = tf.nn.relu(z2)
    #layer3
    z3 = tf.nn.xw_plus_b(z2,w3,b3)

    #output
    y = tf.nn.sigmoid(z3)
    return y
```

We now pass the concatenated feature vectors of the support and query sets to the relation function and get the relation scores:

```
relation_scores = relation_function(Z)
```

We compute `loss_function` as MSE, which is `squared_difference` between `relation_scores` and the actual `y` value:

```
loss_function = tf.reduce_mean(tf.squared_difference(relation_scores,y))
```

We can minimize the loss using `AdamOptimizer`:

```
optimizer = tf.train.AdamOptimizer(0.1)
train = optimizer.minimize(loss_function)
```

Now, let's start our TensorFlow session:

```
sess = tf.InteractiveSession()
sess.run(tf.global_variables_initializer())
```

Now, we randomly sample data points for our support set, `xi`, and query set, `xj`, and train the network:

```
for episode in range(1000):
    _, loss_value = sess.run([train, loss_function],
feed_dict={xi:data[:,0:9]+np.random.randn(*np.shape(data[:,0:9]))*0.05,
xj:data[:,9:]+np.random.randn(*np.shape(data[:,9:]))*0.05,
                                        y:label})
    if episode % 100 == 0:
        print("Episode {}: loss {:.3f} ".format(episode, loss_value))
```

We can see the output as follows:

```
Episode 0: loss 0.495
Episode 100: loss 0.250
Episode 200: loss 0.250
Episode 300: loss 0.250
Episode 400: loss 0.250
Episode 500: loss 0.250
Episode 600: loss 0.250
Episode 700: loss 0.250
Episode 800: loss 0.250
Episode 900: loss 0.250
```

Matching networks

Matching networks are yet another simple and efficient one-shot learning algorithm published by Google's DeepMind team. It can even produce labels for the unobserved class in the dataset.

Let's say we have a support set, S, containing K examples as $(x_1, y_1), (x_2, y_2) \ldots (x_k, y_k)$. When given a query point (a new unseen example), $\hat{x}$, the matching network predicts the class of $\hat{x}$ by comparing it with the support set.

We can define this as $p(\hat{y}|\hat{x}, S)$, where p is the parameterized neural network, $\hat{y}$ is the predicted class for the query point, $\hat{x}$, and S is the support set. $p(\hat{y}|\hat{x}, S)$ will return the probability of $\hat{x}$ belonging to each of the classes in the dataset. Then, we select the class of $\hat{x}$ as the one that has the highest probability. But how does this work exactly? How is this probability computed? Let's us see that now.

The output, $\hat{y}$, for the query point, $\hat{x}$, can be predicted as follows:

$$\hat{y} = \sum_{i=1}^{k} a(\hat{x}, x_i) y_i$$

Let's decipher this equation. x_i and y_i are the input and labels of the support set. $\hat{x}$ is the query input— the input to which we want to predict the label. a is the attention mechanism between $\hat{x}$ and x_i. But how do we perform attention? Here we use a simple attention mechanism, which is the softmax function over the cosine distance between $\hat{x}$ and x_i—that is, $a(\hat{x}, x_i) = softmax(cosine(\hat{x}, x_i))$.

We can't calculate the cosine distance between the raw input, $\hat{x}$ and x_i, directly. So, first, we will learn their embeddings and calculate the cosine distance between the embeddings. We use two different embeddings, f and g, for learning the embeddings of the query input, $\hat{x}$ and support set input, x_i, respectively. We will see how exactly these two embedding functions, f and g, learn the embeddings in the upcoming section.

So, we can rewrite our attention equation as follows:

$$a(\hat{x}, x_i) = softmax(cosine(f(\hat{x}), g(x_i)))$$

We can rewrite the previous equation as follows:

$$a(\hat{x}, x_i) = \frac{e^{cosine(f(\hat{x}), g(x_i))}}{\sum_{j=1}^{k} e^{cosine(f(\hat{x}), g(x_j))}}$$

So, after calculating the attention matrix, $a(\hat{x}, x_i)$, we multiply our attention matrix with the support set labels, y_i. But how can we multiply the support set labels with our attention matrix? First, we convert our support set labels into one-hot encoded values and then multiply them with our attention matrix and, as a result, we get the probability of $\hat{y}$ belonging to each of the classes in the support set. Then, we apply argmax and select $\hat{y}$ as the one that has a maximum probability value.

Are you still not clear about matching networks? Look at the following diagram; as you can see, we have three classes in our support set, *{lion, elephant and dog}*, and we have a new query image, $\hat{x}$. First, we feed the support set to embedding function, g, and the query image to embedding function, f, and learn their embeddings and calculate the cosine distance between them; then, we apply softmax attention over this cosine distance. Then, we multiply our attention matrix with the one-hot encoded support set labels and get the probabilities, and then we select $\hat{y}$ as the one that has the highest probability. As you can see in the following diagram, the query set image is an elephant, and we have a high probability at the index 1, so we predict the class of $\hat{y}$ as 1 (elephant):

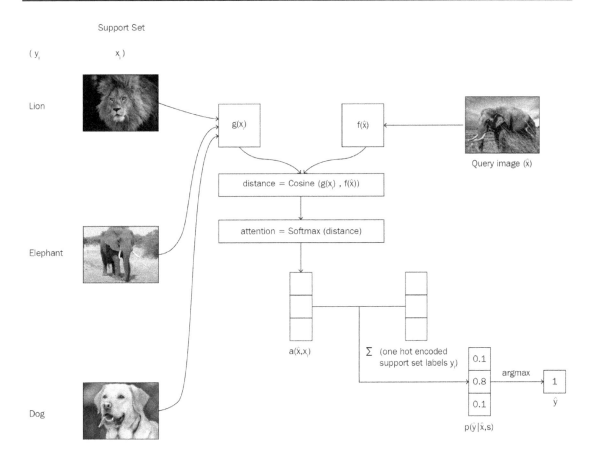

Embedding functions

We have learned that we use two embedding functions, f and g, for learning the embeddings of $\hat{x}$ and x_i respectively. Now we will see exactly how these two functions learn the embeddings.

The support set embedding function (g)

We use the embedding function, g, for learning the embeddings of the support set. We use bidirectional LSTM as our embedding function, g.

We can define our embedding function, g, as follows:

```
def g(X):
    #forward cell
    forward_cell = rnn.BasicLSTMCell(32)

    #backward cell
    backward_cell = rnn.BasicLSTMCell(32)
    #bidirectional LSTM
    outputs, state_forward, state_backward =
rnn.static_bidirectional_rnn(forward_cell, backward_cell, X,
dtype=tf.float32)

    return tf.add(tf.stack(X), tf.stack(outputs))
```

The query set embedding function (f)

We use the embedding function, f, for learning the embedding of our query point, $\hat{x}$. We use LSTM as our encoding function. Along with $\hat{x}$ as the input, we will also pass the embedding of our support set embeddings, which is g(x), and we will pass one more parameter called K, which defines the number of processing steps. Let's see how we compute query set embeddings step-by-step.

First, we will initialize our LSTM cell:

```
cell = rnn.BasicLSTMCell(64)
previous_state = cell.zero_state(batch_size, tf.float32)
```

Then, for the number of processing steps, we do the following:

```
for step in xrange(K):
```

We calculate embeddings of the query set, $\hat{x}$, by feeding it to the LSTM cell:

```
output, state = cell(XHat, previous_state)
h_k = tf.add(output, XHat)
```

Now, we perform softmax attention over the support set embeddings—that is, g_embedings. It helps us to avoid elements that are not required:

```
content_based_attention = tf.nn.softmax(tf.multiply(previous_state[1],
g_embedding))
        r_k = tf.reduce_sum(tf.multiply(content_based_attention, g_embedding),
axis=0)
```

We update previous_state and repeat these steps for a number of processing steps, K:

```
previous_state = rnn.LSTMStateTuple(state[0], tf.add(h_k, r_k))
```

The complete code for computing f_embeddings is given as follows:

```
def f(XHat, g_embedding, K):

    cell = rnn.BasicLSTMCell(64)
    previous_state = cell.zero_state(batch_size, tf.float32)

    for step in xrange(K):
        output, state = cell(XHat, previous_state)
        h_k = tf.add(output, XHat)
        #Soft max attention
        content_based_attention =
tf.nn.softmax(tf.multiply(previous_state[1], g_embedding))
        r_k = tf.reduce_sum(tf.multiply(content_based_attention,
g_embedding), axis=0)

        previous_state = rnn.LSTMStateTuple(state[0], tf.add(h_k, r_k))

    return output
```

The architecture of matching networks

The overall flow of matching network is shown in the following diagram and it is different from the image we saw already. You can notice how the support set, x_i, and query set, $\hat{x}$, are calculated through the embedding functions, g and f, respectively. As you can see, the embedding function, f, takes the query set along with the support set embeddings as input:

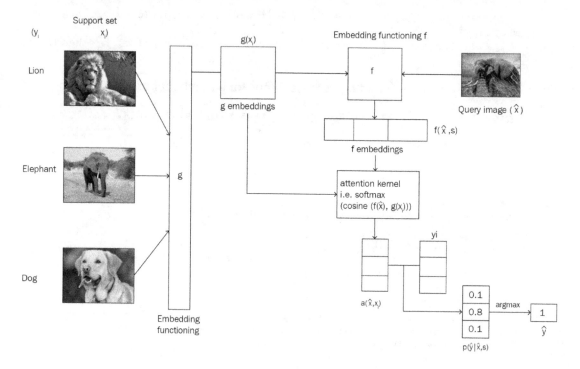

Matching networks in TensorFlow

Now, we will see how to build a matching network in TensorFlow step by step. We will see the final code at the end.

First, we import the libraries:

```
import tensorflow as tf
slim = tf.contrib.slim
rnn = tf.contrib.rnn
```

Now, we define a class called `Matching_network`, where we define our network:

```
class Matching_network():
```

We define the __init__ method, where we initialize all of the variables:

```
def __init__(self, lr, n_way, k_shot, batch_size=32):
    #placeholder for support set
    self.support_set_image = tf.placeholder(tf.float32, [None, n_way *
k_shot, 28, 28, 1])
    self.support_set_label = tf.placeholder(tf.int32, [None, n_way *
k_shot, ])
    #placeholder for query set
    self.query_image = tf.placeholder(tf.float32, [None, 28, 28, 1])
    self.query_label = tf.placeholder(tf.int32, [None, ])
```

Let's say our support set and query set have images. Before feeding this raw image to the embedding function, first, we will extract the features from the image using a convolutional network and then we feed the extracted features of the support set and query set to the embedding functions of *g* and *f* respectively.

So, we will define a function called `image_encoder`, which is used for encoding features from the image. We use a four-layered convolutional network with a max pooling operation as our image encoder:

```
def image_encoder(self, image):
    with slim.arg_scope([slim.conv2d], num_outputs=64, kernel_size=3,
normalizer_fn=slim.batch_norm):
        #conv1
        net = slim.conv2d(image)
        net = slim.max_pool2d(net, [2, 2])
        #conv2
        net = slim.conv2d(net)
        net = slim.max_pool2d(net, [2, 2])
        #conv3
        net = slim.conv2d(net)
        net = slim.max_pool2d(net, [2, 2])
        #conv4
        net = slim.conv2d(net)
        net = slim.max_pool2d(net, [2, 2])
    return tf.reshape(net, [-1, 1 * 1 * 64])
```

Now we define our embedding functions; we have already seen how the embedding functions, *f* and *g*, are defined in the *Embedding function* section. So, we can define them directly as follows:

```
#embedding function for extracting support set embeddings
    def g(self, x_i):

        forward_cell = rnn.BasicLSTMCell(32)
        backward_cell = rnn.BasicLSTMCell(32)
        outputs, state_forward, state_backward =
rnn.static_bidirectional_rnn(forward_cell, backward_cell, x_i,
dtype=tf.float32)

        return tf.add(tf.stack(x_i), tf.stack(outputs))

    #embedding function for extracting query set embeddings
    def f(self, XHat, g_embedding):
        cell = rnn.BasicLSTMCell(64)
        prev_state = cell.zero_state(self.batch_size, tf.float32)

        for step in xrange(self.processing_steps):
            output, state = cell(XHat, prev_state)
            h_k = tf.add(output, XHat)

            content_based_attention =
tf.nn.softmax(tf.multiply(prev_state[1], g_embedding))
            r_k = tf.reduce_sum(tf.multiply(content_based_attention,
g_embedding), axis=0)

            prev_state = rnn.LSTMStateTuple(state[0], tf.add(h_k, r_k))

        return output
```

Now, we define a function called `cosine_similarity` for learning the cosine similarity between support set and query set embeddings:

```
    def cosine_similarity(self, target, support_set):
        target_normed = target
        sup_similarity = []
        for i in tf.unstack(support_set):
            i_normed = tf.nn.l2_normalize(i, 1)
            similarity = tf.matmul(tf.expand_dims(target_normed, 1),
tf.expand_dims(i_normed, 2))
            sup_similarity.append(similarity)

        return tf.squeeze(tf.stack(sup_similarity, axis=1))
```

Finally, we use a function called `train` to perform our training operation—let's see this step by step:

```
def train(self, support_set_image, support_set_label, query_image):
```

First, we encode the features of support set images using our image encoder:

```
support_set_image_encoded = [self.image_encoder(i) for i in
tf.unstack(support_set_image, axis=1)]
```

Then, we will also encode the features of query set images using the image encoder:

```
query_image_encoded = self.image_encoder(query_image)
```

Next, we will learn the embeddings of our support set using our embedding function, *g*:

```
g_embedding = self.g(support_set_image_encoded)
```

Similarly, we will also learn the embeddings of our query set using our embedding function, *f*:

```
f_embedding = self.f(query_image_encoded, g_embedding)
```

Now, we calculate `cosine_similarity` between both of these embeddings:

```
embeddings_similarity = self.cosine_similarity(f_embedding,
g_embedding)
```

Then, we perform softmax attention over this similarity:

```
attention = tf.nn.softmax(embeddings_similarity)
```

We predict a query set label by multiplying our attention matrix with one-hot encoded support set labels:

```
y_hat = tf.matmul(tf.expand_dims(attention, 1),
tf.one_hot(support_set_label, self.n_way))
```

Next, we get `probabilities`:

```
probabilities = tf.squeeze(y_hat)
```

We select the index that has the highest probability as a class of the query image:

```
predictions = tf.argmax(self.logits, 1)
```

Finally, we define our loss function; we use softmax cross-entropy as our loss function:

```
    loss_function = tf.losses.sparse_softmax_cross_entropy(label,
self.probabilities)
```

We minimize our loss function using `AdamOptimizer`:

```
    tf.train.AdamOptimizer(self.lr).minimize(self.loss_op)
```

Now, we will see the final code of our matching network as a whole:

```
class Matching_network():
    #initialize all the variables
    def __init__(self, lr, n_way, k_shot, batch_size=32):
        #placeholder for support set
        self.support_set_image = tf.placeholder(tf.float32, [None, n_way *
k_shot, 28, 28, 1])
        self.support_set_label = tf.placeholder(tf.int32, [None, n_way *
k_shot, ])
        #placeholder for query set
        self.query_image = tf.placeholder(tf.float32, [None, 28, 28, 1])
        self.query_label = tf.placeholder(tf.int32, [None, ])
    #encoder function for extracting features from the image
    def image_encoder(self, image):
        with slim.arg_scope([slim.conv2d], num_outputs=64, kernel_size=3,
normalizer_fn=slim.batch_norm):
            #conv1
            net = slim.conv2d(image)
            net = slim.max_pool2d(net, [2, 2])
            #conv2
            net = slim.conv2d(net)
            net = slim.max_pool2d(net, [2, 2])
            #conv3
            net = slim.conv2d(net)
            net = slim.max_pool2d(net, [2, 2])
            #conv4
            net = slim.conv2d(net)
            net = slim.max_pool2d(net, [2, 2])
        return tf.reshape(net, [-1, 1 * 1 * 64])
    #embedding function for extracting support set embeddings
    def g(self, x_i):

        forward_cell = rnn.BasicLSTMCell(32)
        backward_cell = rnn.BasicLSTMCell(32)
        outputs, state_forward, state_backward =
rnn.static_bidirectional_rnn(forward_cell, backward_cell, x_i,
dtype=tf.float32)
```

```
        return tf.add(tf.stack(x_i), tf.stack(outputs))

    #embedding function for extracting query set embeddings
    def f(self, XHat, g_embedding):
        cell = rnn.BasicLSTMCell(64)
        prev_state = cell.zero_state(self.batch_size, tf.float32)

        for step in xrange(self.processing_steps):
            output, state = cell(XHat, prev_state)
            h_k = tf.add(output, XHat)

            content_based_attention =
tf.nn.softmax(tf.multiply(prev_state[1], g_embedding))
            r_k = tf.reduce_sum(tf.multiply(content_based_attention,
g_embedding), axis=0)

            prev_state = rnn.LSTMStateTuple(state[0], tf.add(h_k, r_k))

        return output

    #cosine similarity function for calculating cosine similarity between
support set and query set embeddings
    def cosine_similarity(self, target, support_set):
        target_normed = target
        sup_similarity = []
        for i in tf.unstack(support_set):
            i_normed = tf.nn.l2_normalize(i, 1)
            similarity = tf.matmul(tf.expand_dims(target_normed, 1),
tf.expand_dims(i_normed, 2))
            sup_similarity.append(similarity)

        return tf.squeeze(tf.stack(sup_similarity, axis=1))

    def train(self, support_set_image, support_set_label, query_image):
        #encode the features of query set images using our image encoder
        query_image_encoded = self.image_encoder(query_image)
        #encode the features of support set images using our image encoder
        support_set_image_encoded = [self.image_encoder(i) for i in
tf.unstack(support_set_image, axis=1)]
        #generate support set embeddings using our embedding function g
        g_embedding = self.g(support_set_image_encoded)
        #generate query set embeddings using our embedding function f
        f_embedding = self.f(query_image_encoded, g_embedding)

        #calculate the cosine similarity between both of these embeddings
        embeddings_similarity = self.cosine_similarity(f_embedding,
g_embedding)
        #perform attention over the embedding similarity
```

```
        attention = tf.nn.softmax(embeddings_similarity)
        #now predict query set label by multiplying attention matrix with
one hot encoded support set labels
        y_hat = tf.matmul(tf.expand_dims(attention, 1),
tf.one_hot(support_set_label, self.n_way))
        #get the probabilities
        probabilities = tf.squeeze(y_hat)
        #select the index which has the highest probability as a class of
query image
        predictions = tf.argmax(self.probabilities, 1)
        #we use softmax cross entropy loss as our loss function
        loss_function = tf.losses.sparse_softmax_cross_entropy(label,
self.probabilities)
        #we minimize the loss using adam optimizer
        tf.train.AdamOptimizer(self.lr).minimize(self.loss_op)
```

Summary

In this chapter, we have learned how matching networks and relation networks are used in few-shot learning. We saw how a relation network learns the embeddings of the support and query sets and combines the embeddings and feeds them to the relation function to compute the relation score. We also saw how a matching network uses two different embedding functions to learn the embeddings of our support and query sets and how it predicts the class of the query set.

In the next chapter, we will learn how neural Turing machines and memory-augmented neural networks work by storing and retrieving information from the memory.

Questions

1. What are the different types of functions used in relation networks?
2. What is the operator Z in relation networks?
3. What is the relation function?
4. What is the loss function of relation networks?
5. What are the different types of embedding functions used in matching networks?
6. How is the class of the query point predicted in matching networks?

Further reading

- Matching networks: `https://arxiv.org/pdf/1606.04080.pdf`
- Relation networks: `https://arxiv.org/pdf/1711.06025.pdf`

5
Memory-Augmented Neural Networks

So far, in the previous chapters, we have learned several distance-based metric learning algorithms. We started off with siamese networks and saw how siamese networks learn to discriminate between two inputs, then we looked at prototypical networks and variants of prototypical networks, such as Gaussian prototypical networks and semi-prototypical networks. Going ahead, we explored interesting matching networks and relation networks.

In this chapter, we will learn about **Memory-Augmented Neural Networks** (**MANN**), which are used for one-shot learning. Before diving into MANN, we will learn about their predecessor, **Neural Turing Machines** (**NTM**). We will learn how NTMs make use of external memory for storing and retrieving information and we will also see how to use a NTM for perform copy tasks.

In this chapter, we will learn about the following:

- NTM
- Reading and writing in NTM
- Addressing mechanisms
- Copy tasks using NTM
- MANN
- Reading and writing in MANN

NTM

NTM is an interesting algorithm that has the ability to store and retrieve information from memory. The idea of NTM is to augment the neural network with an external memory—that is, instead of using hidden states as a memory, it uses an external memory for storing and retrieving the information. The architecture of NTM is shown in the following figure:

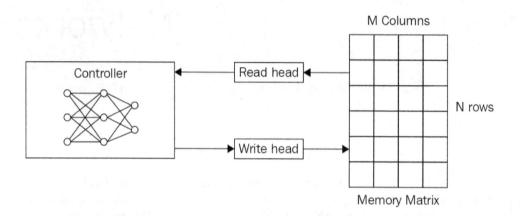

The important components of the NTM are as follows:

- **Controller**: This is basically a feedforward neural network or recurrent neural network. It reads from and writes to the memory.
- **Memory**: The memory matrix or memory bank, or simply the memory, is where we will store the information. Memory is basically a two-dimensional matrix composed of memory cells. The memory matrix contains N rows and M columns. Using the controller, we access the content from the memory. So, the controller receives input from the external environment and emits responses by interacting with the memory matrix.
- **Read and write heads**: The read head and write head are the pointers containing addresses of the memory from which it has to read from and write to.

Okay, but how can we access information from the memory? Can we access the information from the memory by specifying the row and column index? Yes, we can. But the problem is that, if we access information by index, we can't train our NTM using gradient descent because we can't calculate gradients for an index. So, the author of NTM defines blurry operations for reading and writing using a controller. The blurry operation will interact with all of the elements in the memory to some extent. It is basically an attention mechanism that strongly focuses on a particular location in the memory that is important to read/write, while ignoring the focus on the other location. So, we use special read and write operations to determine which location on the memory to focus on. We will explore more on read and write operations in the upcoming section.

Reading and writing in NTM

Now we will see how to read from and write to the memory matrix.

Read operation

A read operation reads a value from the memory. But since we have many memory blocks in our memory matrix, which one do we need to select to read from the memory? That is determined by the weight vector. The weight vector specifies which region in the memory is more important than others. We use an attention mechanism to get this weight vector. We will explore more on how exactly we compute this weight vector in the upcoming section. The weight vector is normalized, meaning that its value ranges from zero to one, and the sum of the value equals one. The following diagram shows the weight vector of the length, N:

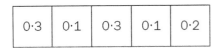

Weight Vector (w_t)

Let's denote this normalized weight vector with w_t, where the subscript, t, implies time and $w_t(i)$ denotes an element in the weight vector at an index, i, and time, t:

$$\sum_i w_t(i) = 1, \qquad 0 \le w_t(i) \le 1, \quad \forall i$$

Our memory matrix consists of N rows and M columns, as shown in the following diagram. Let's represent our memory matrix at the time t as M_t:

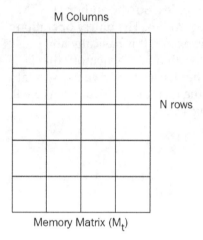

Now that we have the weight vector and memory matrix, we perform a linear combination of a memory matrix, M_t, and a weight vector, w_t, to get the read vector, r_t, as shown in the following figure:

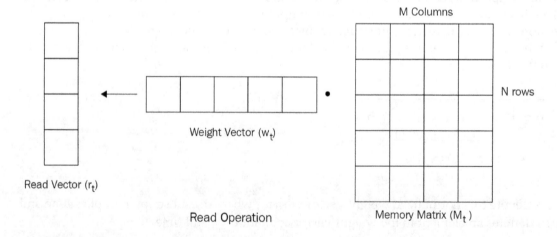

This can be expressed as the following:

$$r_t < -\sum_i w_t(i) M_t(i)$$

As you can see in the preceding figure, we have the memory matrix of the N rows and M columns, and the weight vector of size N containing weights for all of the N locations. Performing a linear combination of these two, we get a read vector of the length M.

Write operation

Unlike read operation, write operation consist of two suboperations called erase and add operations, which erase old information and add new information to the memory, respectively.

Erase operation

We use erase operation to remove information that is not required in the memory. After performing an erase operation, we will have a new updated memory matrix where some elements in the memory would be erased. How can we erase the value of a particular cell in the memory matrix? Here, we introduce one more vector called the erase vector, e_t, of the same length as the weight vector, w_t. The erase vector consist of values of 0s and 1s.

Okay. We have an erase vector. But how can we erase values and get the updated memory matrix? We multiply $(1 - w_t e_t)$ by our memory matrix at a previous step, M_{t-1}, and get the updated memory matrix M_t^*.

That is, $M_t^*(i) < -(1 - w(i)e)M_{t-1}(i)$.

But how does this work? Only if both weight and erase elements at an index i are 1, then that particular element in the memory will be set to 0—in other words, erased; otherwise, it will retain its own value. For example, look at the following diagram. First, we multiply the weight vector, w_t, and erase vector, e_t:

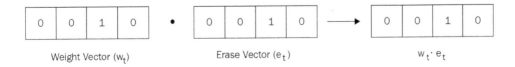

0	0	1	0

Weight Vector (w$_t$)

0	0	1	0

Erase Vector (e$_t$)

0	0	1	0

w$_t$· e$_t$

Then, we subtract 1 from it—that is, $(1 - w_t(i)e_t)$, and we get a new vector as shown in the following:

1	1	0	1

$(1\text{-}w_t \cdot e_t)$

Next, we multiply $(1 - w_t e_t)$ with the memory matrix at the previous time step, M_{t-1}, and get the updated memory matrix, M_t^*:

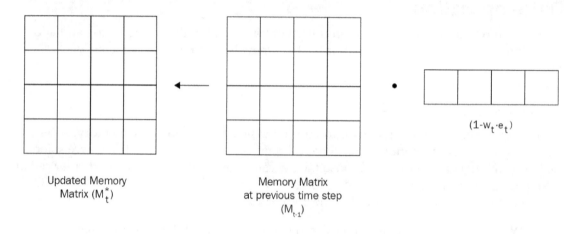

Updated Memory
Matrix (M_t^*)

Memory Matrix
at previous time step
($M_{t\text{-}1}$)

$(1\text{-}w_t \cdot e_t)$

Erase Operation

Add operation

After completing the erase operation, we get the updated memory matrix, M_t^*, where some elements in the memory would be erased. Now, we want to add new information to the memory matrix. How do we do that? We introduce another vector called the add vector, a_t, which has values to be added to the memory. We multiply elements of the weight vector, w_t, and add vector, a_t, and then add them to the memory—that is,

$M_t(i) < -M_t^*(i) + w_t(i)a_t$.

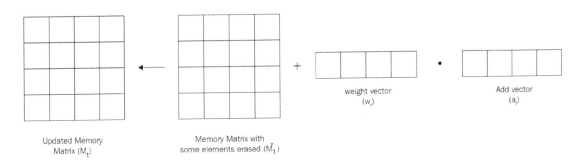

Add operation

Addressing mechanisms

So far, we have seen how to perform read and write operation and we saw how the weight vector is used to perform those operations. But how do we compute this weight vector? We use an attention mechanism and different addressing schemes to compute it. We use two types of addressing mechanisms to access information from the memory:

- Content-based addressing
- Location-based addressing

Content-based addressing

In content-based addressing, we select values from the memory based on similarity. The controller returns a key vector called k_t. We compare this key vector, k_t, with each of the rows in the memory matrix ,M_t, to learn the similarity. We use cosine similarity as a similarity measure for checking the similarity, which can be expressed as follows:

$$cosine[k_t, M_t] = \frac{k_t . M_t}{|k_t| . |M_t|}$$

We introduce a new parameter called β, which is called the key strength. It determines how concentrated our weight vector should be. Based on the value of β, we can increase or decrease the focus—that is, we can tune our attention to a particular location based on the value of the key strength, β. When the value of β is low, we focus on all of the locations equally; when the value of β is high, we focus on a particular location.

So, our weight vector becomes the following:

$$w_t^c = \beta_t \ cosine[k_t, M_t(i)]$$

That is, the cosine similarity between key vector, k_t, and memory matrix, M_t, multiplied by the key strength β. The superscript c in w_t^c denotes that they are content-based weights. Instead of using this directly, we apply softmax over the weights. So, our final weights become as follows:

$$w_t^c = \frac{exp(\beta_t \ cosine[k_t, M_t(i)])}{\sum_j exp(\beta_t \ cosine[k_t, M_t(j)])}$$

Location-based addressing

Unlike content-based addressing, in location-based addressing, we focus on the location and not on the content similarity. It consists of three steps:

1. Interpolation
2. Convolution shift
3. Sharpening

Interpolation

The first step in location-based addressing is called interpolation. It is used to decide whether we should use the weights we obtained at the previous time step ,w_{t-1}, or use the weights obtained through content-based addressing, w_t^c. But how do we decide that? We use a new scalar parameter, g_t, which is used for determining which weights we should use. The value of g_t can be either 0 or 1.

We can express our weight vector calculation as follows:

$$w_t^g < -g_t w_t^c + (1 - g_t)w_{t-1}$$

- When the value of g_t is 0, our equation becomes $w_t^g < -w_{t-1}$, which implies our weight vector is the one we obtained at the previous time step.
- When the value of g_t is 1, our equation becomes $w_t^g < -w_t^c$, which implies our weight vector is the one we obtained through content-based addressing.

So the value of g_t acts as a gate to switch between which weights we have to use.

Convolution shift

The next step is called convolution shift. It is used for moving the head position. That is, it is used for shifting the focus from one location to the another. Each head emits a parameter called a shift weight s_t, which give us a distribution over which allowable integer shifts are performed. For example, let's say we have shifts between -1 and 1 that are allowed, then a length of s_t would become three, comprising *{-1,0,1}*.

So, what exactly do these shifts mean? Let's say we have three elements in our weight vector, w_t^g—that is, $w_t^g = [w_{i-1}^g, w_i^g, w_{i+1}^g]$, and we have three elements in the shift weight vector—that is, $s_t = [-1, 0, 1]$.

A shift of -1 means that we will shift the element in w_t^g from left to right. A shift of 0 keeps the element at the same position and a shift of +1 means that we will shift the element from right to left. This can be seen in the following diagram:

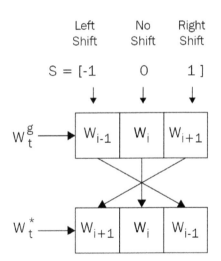

Now, look at the following diagram where we have shift weights $s_t = [1, 0, 0]$, meaning that we perform a left shift, as shift values are 0 at other positions:

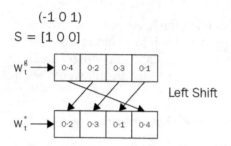

Similarly, when $s_t = [0, 0, 1]$ we perform a right shift, as shift values are 0 at other positions, as shown in the following diagram:

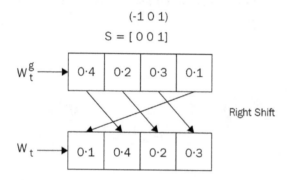

So, in this way, we perform convolution shifts over elements in the weight matrix. If we 0 to *N-1* memory locations, then we can express our convolution shift as follows:

$$w_t^*(i) < -\sum_{j=0}^{N-1} w_t^g(j) s_t(i - j)$$

```
erase_add_list = tf.split(parameters[:, num_parameters_per_head *
num_heads:], 2 * self.write_head_num, axis=1)
```

Next, we get the previous weight vector and the previous memory:

```
#previous weight vector
prev_w_list = prev_state['w_list']

#previous memory
prev_M = prev_state['M']

w_list = []
p_list = []
```

Now, we will initialize some of the important parameters that we use for addressing:

```
for i, head_parameter in enumerate(head_parameter_list):

    #key vector
    k = tf.tanh(head_parameter[:, 0:self.memory_vector_dim])

    #key strength(beta)
    beta = tf.sigmoid(head_parameter[:, self.memory_vector_dim]) * 10

    #interpolation gate
    g = tf.sigmoid(head_parameter[:, self.memory_vector_dim + 1])

    #shift matrix
    s = tf.nn.softmax(
        head_parameter[:, self.memory_vector_dim + 2:self.memory_vector_dim
+ 2 + (self.shift_range * 2 + 1)]
    )

    #sharpening factor
    gamma = tf.log(tf.exp(head_parameter[:, -1]) + 1) + 1

    with tf.variable_scope('addressing_head_%d' % i):
        w = self.addressing(k, beta, g, s, gamma, prev_M, prev_w_list[i])

    w_list.append(w)
    p_list.append({'k': k, 'beta': beta, 'g': g, 's': s, 'gamma': gamma})
```

Read operations:

Select the read head as follows:

```
read_w_list = w_list[:self.read_head_num]
```

We know that the read operation is the linear combination of weights and memory:

```
read_vector_list = []
for i in range(self.read_head_num):

    #linear combination of the weights and memory
    read_vector = tf.reduce_sum(tf.expand_dims(read_w_list[i], dim=2) *
prev_M, axis=1)
    read_vector_list.append(read_vector)
```

Write operations:

Unlike the read operation, a write operation involves two steps, erase and add.

Select the head to write as follows:

```
write_w_list = w_list[self.read_head_num:]

#update the memory
M = prev_M
```

Perform the erase and add operations:

```
for i in range(self.write_head_num):

    #the erase vector will be multipled with weight vector to denote which
location to erase or keep unchanged
    w = tf.expand_dims(write_w_list[i], axis=2)
    erase_vector = tf.expand_dims(tf.sigmoid(erase_add_list[i * 2]),
axis=1)

    #next we perform the add operation
    add_vector = tf.expand_dims(tf.tanh(erase_add_list[i * 2 + 1]), axis=1)
    M = M * (tf.ones(M.get_shape()) - tf.matmul(w, erase_vector)) +
tf.matmul(w, add_vector)
```

Get the controller output:

```
if not self.output_dim:
    output_dim = x.get_shape()[1]
else:
    output_dim = self.output_dim

with tf.variable_scope("o2o", reuse=(self.step > 0) or self.reuse):
    o2o_w = tf.get_variable('o2o_w', [controller_output.get_shape()[1],
output_dim],
initializer=tf.random_normal_initializer(mean=0.0, stddev=0.5))
    o2o_b = tf.get_variable('o2o_b', [output_dim],
```

```
        initializer=tf.random_normal_initializer(mean=0.0, stddev=0.5))
            NTM_output = tf.nn.xw_plus_b(controller_output, o2o_w, o2o_b)

    state = {
        'controller_state': controller_state,
        'read_vector_list': read_vector_list,
        'w_list': w_list,
        'p_list': p_list,
        'M': M
    }

    self.step += 1
```

Addressing mechanisms:

As we know we use two types of addressing—content-based and location-based.

Content-based addressing:

Compute the cosine similarity between the key vector and memory matrix:

```
k = tf.expand_dims(k, axis=2)
inner_product = tf.matmul(prev_M, k)

k_norm = tf.sqrt(tf.reduce_sum(tf.square(k), axis=1, keepdims=True))
M_norm = tf.sqrt(tf.reduce_sum(tf.square(prev_M), axis=2, keepdims=True))
norm_product = M_norm * k_norm

K = tf.squeeze(inner_product / (norm_product + 1e-8))
```

Now, we produce the normalized weight vector based on the similarity and the key strength (beta). Beta is used for adjusting the precision on the head focus:

```
K_amplified = tf.exp(tf.expand_dims(beta, axis=1) * K)
w_c = K_amplified / tf.reduce_sum(K_amplified, axis=1, keepdims=True)  # eq
(5)
```

Location-based addressing:

Location-based addressing involves three other steps:

1. Interpolation
2. Convolutional shift
3. Sharpening

Interpolation:

This is used to decide whether we should use the weights we obtained at the previous time step, `prev_w`, or use the weights obtained through content-based addressing, `w_c`. But how do we decide that? We use a new scalar parameter, `g`, which is used for determining which weights we should use:

```
g = tf.expand_dims(g, axis=1)
w_g = g * w_c + (1 - g) * prev_w
```

Convolutional shift:

After interpolation, we perform a convolutional shift so that the controller can focus on the other rows:

```
s = tf.concat([s[:, :self.shift_range + 1],
                tf.zeros([s.get_shape()[0], self.memory_size -
(self.shift_range * 2 + 1)]),
                s[:, -self.shift_range:]], axis=1)

t = tf.concat([tf.reverse(s, axis=[1]), tf.reverse(s, axis=[1])], axis=1)

s_matrix = tf.stack(
    [t[:, self.memory_size - i - 1:self.memory_size * 2 - i - 1] for i in
range(self.memory_size)],
    axis=1
)

w_ = tf.reduce_sum(tf.expand_dims(w_g, axis=1) * s_matrix, axis=2) # eq (8)
```

Sharpening:

Finally, we perform a sharpening operation to prevent the shifted weight vectors from blurring:

```
w_sharpen = tf.pow(w_, tf.expand_dims(gamma, axis=1))
w = w_sharpen / tf.reduce_sum(w_sharpen, axis=1, keepdims=True)
```

Next, we define the function called `zero_state` for initializing all of the states of a controller, read vector, weights, and memory:

```
def zero_state(self, batch_size, dtype):
    def expand(x, dim, N):
        return tf.concat([tf.expand_dims(x, dim) for _ in range(N)],
axis=dim)
```

```
            with tf.variable_scope('init', reuse=self.reuse):
                state = {
                    'controller_state':
    expand(tf.tanh(tf.get_variable('init_state', self.rnn_size,
    initializer=tf.random_normal_initializer(mean=0.0, stddev=0.5))),
                                    dim=0, N=batch_size),
                    'read_vector_list':
    [expand(tf.nn.softmax(tf.get_variable('init_r_%d' % i,
    [self.memory_vector_dim],
    initializer=tf.random_normal_initializer(mean=0.0, stddev=0.5))),
                                    dim=0, N=batch_size)
                            for i in range(self.read_head_num)],
                    'w_list': [expand(tf.nn.softmax(tf.get_variable('init_w_%d'
    % i, [self.memory_size],
    initializer=tf.random_normal_initializer(mean=0.0, stddev=0.5))),
                                    dim=0, N=batch_size) if
    self.addressing_mode == 'content_and_loaction'
                                else tf.zeros([batch_size, self.memory_size])
                                for i in range(self.read_head_num +
    self.write_head_num)],
                    'M': expand(tf.tanh(tf.get_variable('init_M',
    [self.memory_size, self.memory_vector_dim],
    initializer=tf.random_normal_initializer(mean=0.0, stddev=0.5))),
                                    dim=0, N=batch_size)
                }
                return state
```

Next, we define a function called `generate_random_strings`, which generates a random sequence of the length, `seq_length`, and we will feed those sequence to the NTM input for the copy task:

```
def generate_random_strings(batch_size, seq_length, vector_dim):
    return np.random.randint(0, 2, size=[batch_size, seq_length,
vector_dim]).astype(np.float32)
```

Now, we create `NTMCopyModel` to perform the whole copy task:

```
class NTMCopyModel():
    def __init__(self, args, seq_length, reuse=False):
        #input sequence
        self.x = tf.placeholder(name='x', dtype=tf.float32,
shape=[args.batch_size, seq_length, args.vector_dim])
        #output sequence
        self.y = self.x
        #end of the sequence
        eof = np.zeros([args.batch_size, args.vector_dim + 1])
        eof[:, args.vector_dim] = np.ones([args.batch_size])
        eof = tf.constant(eof, dtype=tf.float32)
```

```
            zero = tf.constant(np.zeros([args.batch_size, args.vector_dim +
1]), dtype=tf.float32)
        if args.model == 'LSTM':
            def rnn_cell(rnn_size):
                return tf.nn.rnn_cell.BasicLSTMCell(rnn_size, reuse=reuse)
            cell = tf.nn.rnn_cell.MultiRNNCell([rnn_cell(args.rnn_size) for
_ in range(args.rnn_num_layers)])
        elif args.model == 'NTM':
            cell = NTMCell(args.rnn_size, args.memory_size,
args.memory_vector_dim, 1, 1,
                                    addressing_mode='content_and_location',
                                    reuse=reuse,
                                    output_dim=args.vector_dim)
        #initialize all the states
        state = cell.zero_state(args.batch_size, tf.float32)
        self.state_list = [state]
        for t in range(seq_length):
            output, state = cell(tf.concat([self.x[:, t, :],
np.zeros([args.batch_size, 1])], axis=1), state)
            self.state_list.append(state)
        #get the output and states
        output, state = cell(eof, state)
        self.state_list.append(state)

        self.o = []
        for t in range(seq_length):
            output, state = cell(zero, state)
            self.o.append(output[:, 0:args.vector_dim])
            self.state_list.append(state)
        self.o = tf.sigmoid(tf.transpose(self.o, perm=[1, 0, 2]))

        eps = 1e-8
        #calculate loss as cross entropy loss
        self.copy_loss = -tf.reduce_mean(self.y * tf.log(self.o + eps) + (1
- self.y) * tf.log(1 - self.o + eps))
        #optimize using RMS prop optimizer
        with tf.variable_scope('optimizer', reuse=reuse):
            self.optimizer =
tf.train.RMSPropOptimizer(learning_rate=args.learning_rate, momentum=0.9,
decay=0.95)
            gvs = self.optimizer.compute_gradients(self.copy_loss)
            capped_gvs = [(tf.clip_by_value(grad, -10., 10.), var) for
grad, var in gvs]
            self.train_op = self.optimizer.apply_gradients(capped_gvs)
        self.copy_loss_summary = tf.summary.scalar('copy_loss_%d' %
seq_length, self.copy_loss)
```

We reset our TensorFlow graph with the following command:

```
tf.reset_default_graph()
```

Then, we define all of the arguments as follows:

```
parser = argparse.ArgumentParser()
parser.add_argument('--mode', default="train")
parser.add_argument('--restore_training', default=False)
parser.add_argument('--test_seq_length', type=int, default=5)
parser.add_argument('--model', default="NTM")
parser.add_argument('--rnn_size', default=16)
parser.add_argument('--rnn_num_layers', default=3)
parser.add_argument('--max_seq_length', default=5)
parser.add_argument('--memory_size', default=16)
parser.add_argument('--memory_vector_dim', default=5)
parser.add_argument('--batch_size', default=5)
parser.add_argument('--vector_dim', default=8)
parser.add_argument('--shift_range', default=1)
parser.add_argument('--num_epoches', default=100)
parser.add_argument('--learning_rate', default=1e-4)
parser.add_argument('--save_dir', default= os.getcwd())
parser.add_argument('--tensorboard_dir', default=os.getcwd())
args = parser.parse_args(args = [])
```

Finally, we define our `training` function:

```
def train(args):
    model_list = [NTMCopyModel(args, 1)]
    for seq_length in range(2, args.max_seq_length + 1):
        model_list.append(NTMCopyModel(args, seq_length, reuse=True))

    with tf.Session() as sess:
        if args.restore_training:
            saver = tf.train.Saver()
            ckpt = tf.train.get_checkpoint_state(args.save_dir + '/' +
args.model)
            saver.restore(sess, ckpt.model_checkpoint_path)
        else:
            saver = tf.train.Saver(tf.global_variables())
            tf.global_variables_initializer().run()
        #initialize summary writer for visualizing in tensorboard
        train_writer = tf.summary.FileWriter(args.tensorboard_dir,
sess.graph)
        plt.ion()
        plt.show()
        for b in range(args.num_epoches):
            #initialize the sequence length
```

```
            seq_length = np.random.randint(1, args.max_seq_length + 1)
            model = model_list[seq_length - 1]
            #generate our random input sequence as an input
            x = generate_random_strings(args.batch_size, seq_length,
args.vector_dim)
            #feed our input to the model
            feed_dict = {model.x: x}
            if b % 100 == 0:
                p = 0
                print("First training batch sample",x[p, :, :])
                #compute model output
                print("Model output",sess.run(model.o,
feed_dict=feed_dict)[p, :, :])
                state_list = sess.run(model.state_list,
feed_dict=feed_dict)
                if args.model == 'NTM':
                    w_plot = []
                    M_plot = np.concatenate([state['M'][p, :, :] for state
in state_list])
                    for state in state_list:
                        w_plot.append(np.concatenate([state['w_list'][0][p,
:], state['w_list'][1][p, :]]))
                    #plot the weight matrix to see the attention
                    plt.imshow(w_plot, interpolation='nearest',
cmap='gray')
                    plt.draw()
                    plt.pause(0.001)
                #compute loss
                copy_loss = sess.run(model.copy_loss, feed_dict=feed_dict)
                #write to summary
                merged_summary = sess.run(model.copy_loss_summary,
feed_dict=feed_dict)
                train_writer.add_summary(merged_summary, b)
                print('batches %d, loss %g' % (b, copy_loss))
            else:
                sess.run(model.train_op, feed_dict=feed_dict)
            #save the model
            if b % 5000 == 0 and b > 0:
                saver.save(sess, args.save_dir + '/' + args.model +
'/model.tfmodel', global_step=b)
```

Then, we start training the NTM with the following command:

```
train(args)
```

We can see the output as follows, where we can see attention focused on the weight matrix:

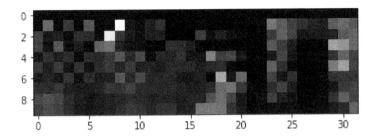

Memory-augmented neural networks (MANN)

Now we will see an interesting variant of NTM, called MANN. It is extensively used for one-shot learning tasks. MANN is designed to make NTM perform better at one-shot learning tasks. We know that NTM can either use content-based addressing or location-based addressing. But in MANN, we use only content-based addressing.

MANN uses a new addressing scheme called least recently used access. As the name suggests, it writes to the least recently used memory location. Wait. What? We just learned that MANN is not location-based, so why are we writing to the least recently used location? This is because the least recently used memory location is determined by the read operation and the read operation is performed by content-based addressing. So, we basically perform content-based addressing for reading and write to the location that was least recently used.

Read and write operations

Now we will see how to perform read and write operations in MANN and how they differ from NTM.

Read operation

Unlike NTM, in MANN, we use two different weight vectors to perform read and write operations. Read operations in MANN are the same as the NTM. Since we know that, in MANN, we perform read operation using content-based similarity, we compare the key vector, k_t, emitted by a controller with each of the rows in the memory matrix, M_t, to learn the similarity. We use cosine similarity as a similarity measure for checking the similarity and can be expressed as follows:

$$cosine[k_t, M_t] = \frac{k_t \cdot M_t}{|k_t| \cdot |M_t|}$$

So, our weight vector becomes as follows:

$$w_t^r = cosine[k_t, M_t(i)]$$

But, unlike NTM, we don't use the key strength, β, here. The superscript r in w_t^r denotes that it is a read weight vector. Our final weight vector is the softmax over the weights—that is, the following:

$$w_t^r = \frac{exp(cosine[k_t, M_t(i)])}{\sum_j exp(cosine[k_t, M_t(j)])}$$

Our read vector is the linear combination of weights, w_t^r, and memory matrix, M_t, as follows:

$$r_t < -\sum_i^R w_t^r(i) M_t(i)$$

Let's see how to build this is in TensorFlow.

First, we calculate read weight vector using content-based similarity:

```
def read_head_addressing(k, prev_M):
    k = tf.expand_dims(k, axis=2)
    inner_product = tf.matmul(prev_M, k)
    k_norm = tf.sqrt(tf.reduce_sum(tf.square(k), axis=1,
keep_dims=True))
    M_norm = tf.sqrt(tf.reduce_sum(tf.square(prev_M), axis=2,
keep_dims=True))
    norm_product = M_norm * k_norm
    K = tf.squeeze(inner_product / (norm_product + 1e-8))
```

```
K_exp = tf.exp(K)
w = K_exp / tf.reduce_sum(K_exp, axis=1, keep_dims=True)
return w
```

Then, we get the read weight vector:

```
w_r = read_head_addressing(k, prev_M)
```

We perform the read operation, which is the linear combination of the read weight vector and memory:

```
read_vector_list = []
    with tf.variable_scope('reading'):
        for i in range(self.head_num):
            read_vector = tf.reduce_sum(tf.expand_dims(w_r_list[i],
dim=2) * M, axis=1)
            read_vector_list.append(read_vector)
```

Write operation

Before performing a write operation, we want to find the least recently used memory location because that is where we have to write. How can we find the least recently used memory location? To find that, we compute a new vector called the usage weight vector. It is denoted by w_t^u and will be updated after every read and write step. It is just a sum of the read weight vector and write weight vector—that is, $w_t^u < -w_t^r + w_t^w$.

Along with adding read and weight vectors, we update our usage weight vector by adding the decaying previous usage weight vector, w_{t-1}^u. We use the decay parameter called γ, which is used to determine how previous usage weights have to be decayed. So, our final usage weight vector is the sum of the decaying previous usage weight vector, read weight vector, and write weight vector:

$$w_t^u < -\gamma w_{t-1}^u + w_t^r + w_t^w$$

Now that we calculated the usage weight vector, how can we compute the least recently used location? For that, we introduce one more weight vector, called the least used weight vector, w_t^{lu}.

Computing least used weight vector, w_t^{lu}, from the usage weight vector, w_t^u, is very simple. We simply set the index of the lowest value in the usage weight vector to 1 and the rest of the values to 0, as the lowest value in the usage weight vector means that it is least recently used:

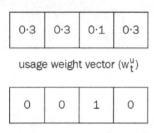

0·3	0·3	0·1	0·3

usage weight vector (w$_t^u$)

0	0	1	0

Least used weight vector (w$_t^w$)

Okay, what's next? We have computed the least used weight vector. Now, how do we compute the write weight vector ,w_t^w? We compute the write weight vector using a sigmoid gate, which is used to compute a convex combination of the previous read weight vector, w_{t-1}^r, and previous least used weight vector w_{t-1}^{lu}:

$$w_t^w < -\sigma(\alpha)w_{t-1}^r + (1 - \sigma(\alpha))w_{t-1}^{lu}$$

After computing the write weight vector, we finally update our memory matrix:

$$M_t(i) < -M_{t-1}(i) + w_t^w(i)k_t$$

We will see how to build this in TensorFlow.

We compute the usage weight vector:

```
w_u = self.gamma * prev_w_u + tf.add_n(w_r_list) + tf.add_n(w_w_list)
```

Then, we compute the least used weight vector:

```
def least_used(w_u):
    _, indices = tf.nn.top_k(w_u, k=self.memory_size)
    w_lu = tf.reduce_sum(tf.one_hot(indices[:, -self.head_num:],
depth=self.memory_size), axis=1)
    return indices, w_lu
```

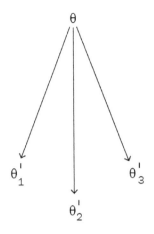

However, instead of initializing θ in a random position—that is, with random values—if we initialize θ in a position that is common to all three tasks, we don't need to take more gradient steps and it will take us less time for training. MAML tries to do exactly this. MAML tries to find this optimal parameter θ that is common to many of the related tasks, so we can train a new task relatively quickly with few data points without having to take many gradient steps.

As shown in the following diagram, we shift θ to a position that is common to all different optimal θ' values:

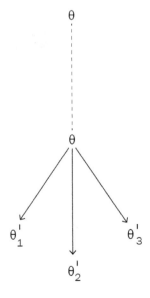

So, for a new related task, say, T_4, we don't have to start with a randomly initialized parameter, θ. Instead, we can start with the optimal θ value so that it will take fewer gradient steps to attain convergence.

So, in MAML, we try to find this optimal θ value that is common to related tasks, so that will help us in learning from fewer data points and minimizing our training time. MAML is model agnostic, meaning that we can apply MAML to any models that are trainable with gradient descent. But how exactly does MAML work? How do we shift the model parameters to an optimal position? We will explore that in detail in the next section.

MAML algorithm

Now that we have a basic understanding of MAML, we will explore it in detail. Let's say we have a model f parameterized by θ—that is, $f_\theta()$—and we have a distribution over tasks, $p(T)$. First, we initialize our parameter θ with some random values. Next, we sample some batch of tasks T_i from a distribution over tasks—that is, $T_i \sim p(T)$. Let's say we have sampled five tasks, $T = \{T_1, T_2, T_3, T_4, T_5\}$, then, for each task T_i, we sample k data points and train the model. We do so by computing the loss $L_{T_i}(f_\theta)$ and we minimize the loss using gradient descent and find the optimal set of parameters that minimize the loss:

$$\theta'_i = \theta - \alpha \nabla_\theta L_{T_i}(f_\theta)$$

In the previous equation, the following applies:

- θ'_i is the optimal parameter for a task T_i
- θ is the initial parameter
- α is the hyperparameter
- $\nabla_\theta L_{T_i}(f_\theta)$ is the gradient of a task T_i

So, after the preceding gradient update, we will have optimal parameters for all five tasks that we have sampled:

$$\theta' = \{\theta'_1, \theta'_2, \theta'_3, \theta'_4, \theta'_5\}$$

Now, before sampling the next batch of tasks, we perform a meta update or meta optimization. That is, in the previous step, we found the optimal parameter θ'_i by training on each of the tasks, T_i. Now we calculate the gradient with respect to these optimal parameters θ'_i and update our randomly initialized parameter θ by training on a new set of tasks, T_i. This makes our randomly initialized parameter θ move to an optimal position where we don't have to take many gradient steps while training on the next batch of tasks. This step is called a meta step, meta update, meta optimization, or meta training. It can be expressed as follows:

$$\theta = \theta - \beta \nabla_\theta \sum_{T_i \sim p(T)} L_{T_i}\left(f_{\theta'_i}\right)$$

In the previous equation, the following applies:

- θ is our initial parameter
- β is the hyperparameter
- $\nabla_\theta \sum_{T_i \sim p(T)} L_{T_i}(f_{\theta'_i})$ is the gradient for each of the new task T_i with respect to parameter θ'_i

If you look at our previous meta update equation closely, we can notice that we are updating our model parameter θ by merely taking an average of gradients of each new task T_i with the optimal parameter θ'_i.

The overall algorithm of MAML is shown in the following diagram; our algorithm consists of two loops—an inner loop where we find the optimal parameter θ'_i for each of the task T_i and an outer loop where we update our randomly initialized model parameter θ by calculating gradients with respect to the optimal parameters θ'_i in a new set of tasks T_i:

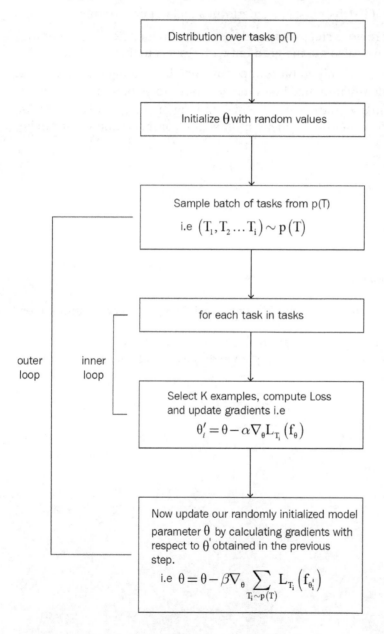

We should always remember that we should not use the same set of tasks T_i with which we find the optimal parameter θ'_i while updating the model parameter θ in the outer loop.

So, in a nutshell, in MAML, we sample a batch of tasks and, for each task T_i in the batch, we minimize the loss using gradient descent and get the optimal parameter θ'_i. Then, before sampling another batch of tasks, we update our randomly initialized model parameter θ by calculating gradients with respect to the optimal parameters θ'_i in a new set of tasks T_i.

MAML in supervised learning

MAML is pretty good at finding the optimal initial parameter, right? Now, we will see how can we use MAML in the supervised learning setting. Before going ahead, let's quickly define our loss functions. Loss function can be any function according to the task we are performing.

If we are performing regression, then we can use our loss function as a mean squared error:

$$L_{T_i}(f_\theta) = \sum_{x_j, y_j \sim T_i} ||f_\theta(x_i) - y_i||_2^2$$

If it is a classification task, then we can use a loss function such as cross-entropy loss:

$$L_{T_i}(f_\theta) = \sum_{x_j, y_j \sim T_i} y_j \log f_\theta(x_j) + (1 - y_j)\log(1 - f_\theta(x_j))$$

Now let's see step-by-step, exactly how MAML is used in supervised learning:

1. Let's say we have a model f parameterized by a parameter θ and we have a distribution over tasks $p(T)$. First, we randomly initialize the model parameter θ.
2. We sample some batch of tasks T_i from a distribution of tasks, that is, $T_i \sim p(T)$. Let's say we have sampled three tasks, then $T = \{T_1, T_2, T_3\}$.

3. **Inner loop**: For each task (T_i) in tasks (T), we sample k data points and prepare our train and test datasets:

$$D_i^{train} = \{(x_1, y_1), (x_2, y_2).\dots.(x_k, y_k)\}$$
$$D_i^{test} = \{(x_1, y_1), (x_2, y_2).\dots.(x_k, y_k)\}$$

Wait! What are the train and test sets? We use the train set in the inner loop for finding the optimal parameters θ'_i and test set in the outer loop for finding the optimal parameter θ. **Test set does not mean that we are checking model's performance. It basically acts as a train set in the outer loop. We can also call our test set as a meta-train set.**

Now we apply any supervised learning algorithm on D_i^{train}, calculate the loss and minimize the loss using gradient descent and get the optimal parameters θ'_i, so $\theta'_i = \theta - \alpha \nabla_\theta L_{T_i}(f_\theta)$. So, for each of the tasks, we sample k data points and minimize the loss on the train set D_i^{train} and get the optimal parameters θ'_i. As we sampled three tasks, we will have three optimal parameters, $\{\theta'_1, \theta'_2, \theta'_3\}$.

4. **Outer loop**: We perform meta optimization in the test set (meta-train set)—that is, here we try to minimize the loss in the test set D_i^{test}. We minimize the loss by calculating the gradient with respect to our optimal parameter θ'_i calculated in the previous step and update our randomly initialized parameter θ using our test set (meta-train set):

$$\theta = \theta - \beta \nabla_\theta \sum_{T_i \sim p(T)} L_{T_i}(f_{\theta'_i})$$

5. We repeat steps 2 to step 5 for n number of iterations. The following diagram gives you an overview of MAML in supervised learning:

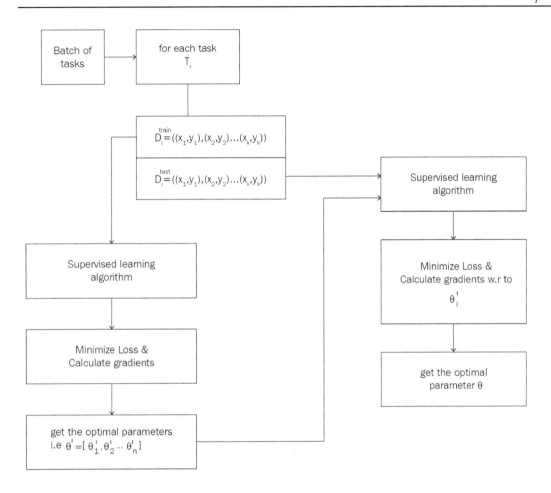

Building MAML from scratch

In the last section, we saw how MAML works. We saw how MAML obtains a better and robust model parameter θ that can be generalizable across tasks. Now we will better understand MAML by coding it from scratch. For better understanding, we will consider a simple binary classification task. We randomly generate our input data and we train it with a simple single layer neural network and try to find the optimal parameter θ. Now, we will see, step-by-step, exactly how to do this:

You can also check the code available as a Jupyter Notebook with an explanation here:
`https://github.com/sudharsan13296/Hands-On-Meta-Learning-With-Python/blob/master/06.%20MAML%20and%20it's%20Variants/6.5%20Building%20MAML%20From%20Scratch.ipynb`.

First, we import the `numpy` library:

```
import numpy as np
```

Generate data points

Now, we define a function called `sample_points` for generating our input (x, y) pairs. It takes the k parameter as input, which implies the number of (x, y) pairs we want to sample:

```
def sample_points(k):
    x = np.random.rand(k,50)
    y = np.random.choice([0, 1], size=k, p=[.5, .5]).reshape([-1,1])
    return x,y
```

The preceding function returns the following output:

```
x, y = sample_points(10)
print x[0]
print y[0]

[0.537339    0.113621    0.62983308 0.3016117   0.91174146 0.95787598
 0.20520229 0.123301    0.64143809 0.68485511 0.29509309 0.65719205
 0.60906626 0.56890899 0.82614517 0.4408421   0.48018921 0.82674918
 0.37076319 0.56239926 0.47655734 0.16489053 0.79742579 0.57731408
 0.62065454 0.70110719 0.61330581 0.84084355 0.7967645   0.84148374
 0.04915798 0.31650656 0.64326928 0.20878387 0.29682973 0.34488916
 0.54626642 0.35608015 0.37950982 0.42281464 0.62984657 0.46538511
 0.84092615 0.38056331 0.21669412 0.44118415 0.65537459 0.2136067
 0.72679706 0.22969462]
[1]
```

Single layer neural network

For simplicity and better understanding, we use a neural network with only a single layer for predicting the output:

```
a = np.matmul(X, theta)
YHat = sigmoid(a)
```

So, we use MAML for finding this optimal parameter value θ that is generalizable across tasks. So, for a new task, we can learn from a few data points in less time by taking fewer gradient steps.

Training using MAML

Now, we define a class called `MAML` where we implement the MAML algorithm. In the
__init__ method, we will initialize all of the necessary variables. Then, we define our
`sigmoid` activation function. Following this we define our `train` function.

We define the class for implementing MAML:

```
class MAML(object):
```

We define the __init__ method and initialize all of the necessary variables:

```
def __init__(self):
```

We initialize a number of tasks—that is, the number of tasks we need in each batch of tasks:

```
self.num_tasks = 10
```

Following is the number of samples—that is, number of shots—a number of data points (k)
we need to have in each task:

```
self.num_samples = 10
```

Following is the number of epochs, that is, training iterations:

```
self.epochs = 1000
```

Following is the hyperparameter for the inner loop (inner gradient update):

```
self.alpha = 0.0001
```

Following is the hyperparameter for the outer loop (outer gradient update)—that is, the
meta optimization:

```
self.beta = 0.0001
```

Then, we randomly initialize our model parameter θ:

```
self.theta = np.random.normal(size=50).reshape(50, 1)
```

We define our `sigmoid` activation function:

```
def sigmoid(self,a):
    return 1.0 / (1 + np.exp(-a))
```

Now, let's get to training:

```
def train(self):
```

For the number of epochs:

```
for e in range(self.epochs):

    self.theta_ = []
```

For task `i` in batch of tasks:

```
for i in range(self.num_tasks):
```

Sample k data points and prepare our train set—that is, D_i^{train}:

```
XTrain, YTrain = sample_points(self.num_samples)
```

We predict the value of `YHat` by a single layer neural network:

```
a = np.matmul(XTrain, self.theta)

YHat = self.sigmoid(a)
```

Since we are performing classification, we use cross entropy loss as our loss function:

```
loss = ((np.matmul(-YTrain.T, np.log(YHat)) - np.matmul((1
-YTrain.T), np.log(1 - YHat)))/self.num_samples)[0][0]
```

We minimize the loss by calculating gradients:

```
gradient = np.matmul(XTrain.T, (YHat - YTrain)) /
self.num_samples
```

We update the gradients and find the optimal parameter θ' for each of tasks T_i, where $\theta'_i = \theta - \alpha \nabla_\theta L_{T_i}(f_\theta)$:

```
self.theta_.append(self.theta - self.alpha*gradient)
```

We initialize the meta gradients:

```
meta_gradient = np.zeros(self.theta.shape)
```

Then we sample k data points and prepare our test set (meta-train set) for meta training—that is, D_i^{test}:

```
for i in range(self.num_tasks):

    XTest, YTest = sample_points(10)
```

We predict the value of YPred by a single layer neural network:

```
a = np.matmul(XTest, self.theta_[i])
YPred = self.sigmoid(a)
```

We compute the meta gradients:

```
meta_gradient += np.matmul(XTest.T, (YPred - YTest)) /
self.num_samples
```

We update our randomly initialized model parameter θ with the meta gradients:

$$\theta = \theta - \beta \nabla_\theta \sum_{T_i \sim p(T)} L_{T_i}(f_{\theta_i'})$$

```
self.theta = self.theta-self.beta*meta_gradient/self.num_tasks
```

We print our loss after every 1,000 epochs:

```
if e%1000==0:
    print "Epoch {}: Loss {}\n".format(e,loss)
    print 'Updated Model Parameter Theta\n'
    print 'Sampling Next Batch of Tasks \n'
    print '---------------------------------\n'
```

The complete code for MAML class is as follows:

```
class MAML(object):
    def __init__(self):
        #initialize number of tasks i.e number of tasks we need in each
batch of tasks
        self.num_tasks = 10
        #number of samples i.e number of shots -number of data points (k)
we need to have in each task
        self.num_samples = 10

        #number of epochs i.e training iterations
        self.epochs = 10000
        #hyperparameter for the inner loop (inner gradient update)
        self.alpha = 0.0001
        #hyperparameter for the outer loop (outer gradient update) i.e meta
optimization
        self.beta = 0.0001
        #randomly initialize our model parameter theta
        self.theta = np.random.normal(size=50).reshape(50, 1)
    #define our sigmoid activation function
    def sigmoid(self,a):
        return 1.0 / (1 + np.exp(-a))
```

```python
            #now let's get to the interesting part i.e training
    def train(self):
        #for the number of epochs,
        for e in range(self.epochs):
            self.theta_ = []
            #for task i in batch of tasks
            for i in range(self.num_tasks):
                #sample k data points and prepare our train set
                XTrain, YTrain = sample_points(self.num_samples)
                a = np.matmul(XTrain, self.theta)

                YHat = self.sigmoid(a)

                #since we are performing classification, we use cross
entropy loss as our loss function
                loss = ((np.matmul(-YTrain.T, np.log(YHat)) - np.matmul((1
-YTrain.T), np.log(1 - YHat)))/self.num_samples)[0][0]
                #minimize the loss by calculating gradients
                gradient = np.matmul(XTrain.T, (YHat - YTrain)) /
self.num_samples

                #update the gradients and find the optimal parameter theta'
for each of tasks
                self.theta_.append(self.theta - self.alpha*gradient)
            #initialize meta gradients
            meta_gradient = np.zeros(self.theta.shape)
            for i in range(self.num_tasks):
                #sample k data points and prepare our test set for meta
training
                XTest, YTest = sample_points(10)

                #predict the value of y
                a = np.matmul(XTest, self.theta_[i])
                YPred = self.sigmoid(a)
                #compute meta gradients
                meta_gradient += np.matmul(XTest.T, (YPred - YTest)) /
self.num_samples

            #update our randomly initialized model parameter theta with the
meta gradients
            self.theta = self.theta-self.beta*meta_gradient/self.num_tasks
            if e%1000==0:
                print "Epoch {}: Loss {}\n".format(e,loss)
                print 'Updated Model Parameter Theta\n'
                print 'Sampling Next Batch of Tasks \n'
                print '---------------------------------\n'
```

Now, let's create an instance to our `MAML` class:

```
model = MAML()
```

We start training the model:

```
model.train()
```

We can see the output as follows; we can notice that the loss drastically reduces from 2.71 on epoch 0 to 0.5 in epoch 3,000:

```
Epoch 0: Loss 2.71883405043

Updated Model Parameter Theta

Sampling Next Batch of Tasks

----------------------------------

Epoch 1000: Loss 1.7829716017

Updated Model Parameter Theta

Sampling Next Batch of Tasks

----------------------------------

Epoch 2000: Loss 1.29532754055

Updated Model Parameter Theta

Sampling Next Batch of Tasks

----------------------------------

Epoch 3000: Loss 0.599713728648

Updated Model Parameter Theta

Sampling Next Batch of Tasks

----------------------------------
```

MAML in reinforcement learning

How can we apply MAML in a **reinforcement learning** (**RL**) setting? In RL, our objective is to find the right policy function that will tell us what actions to perform in each state. But how can we apply meta learning in RL? Let's say we trained our agent to solve the two-armed bandit problem. However, we can't use the same agent to solve the four-armed bandit problem. We have to train the agent again from scratch to solve this new four-armed bandit problem. This is the same case when another *n*-armed bandit comes in. We keep training our agent from scratch to solve new problems even though it is closely related to the problem that the agent has already learned to solve. So, instead of doing this, we can apply meta learning and train our agent on a set of related tasks so that the agent can leverage its previous knowledge to learn new related tasks in minimal time without having to train from scratch.

In RL, we can call a trajectory as a tuple containing a sequence of observations and actions. So, we train our model on these trajectories to learn the optimal policy. But, again, which algorithm should we use to train our model? For MAML, we can use any RL algorithm that can be trained with gradient descent. We use policy gradients for training our model. Policy gradients find the optimal policy by directly parameterizing the policy π with some parameter θ as π_θ. So, using MAML, we try to find this optimal parameter θ that is generalizable across tasks.

But what should our loss function be? In RL, our goal is to find the optimal policy by maximizing positive rewards and minimizing negative rewards, so our loss function becomes minimizing the negative rewards and it can be expressed as follows:

$$L_{T_i}(f_\theta) = -\mathbb{E}_{x_t, a_t \sim f_\theta, qT_i} \left[\sum_{t=1}^{H} R_i(x_t, a_t) \right]$$

But what's going on in the previous equation? $R(x_y, a_t)$ implies the reward for the state x with action a at the time t, and $t=1$ to H implies our time step where H is the horizon—our final time step.

Let's say we have a model *f* parameterized by θ—that is, $f_\theta()$—and distribution over tasks *p(T)*. First, we initialize our parameter θ with some random values. Next, we sample some batch of tasks T_i from a distribution over tasks: $T_i \sim p(T)$.

Then, for each task, we sample k trajectories and build our train and test sets: $D_i^{train}, D_i^{test} \sim T_i$. Our dataset basically contains the trajectory information such as observations and actions. We minimize the loss on the train set D_i^{train} by performing gradient descent and find the optimal parameters θ':

$$\theta'_i = \theta - \alpha \nabla_\theta L_{T_i}(f_\theta)$$

Now, before sampling the next batch of tasks, we perform the meta update—that is, we try to minimize the loss on our test set D_i^{test} by calculating gradients of the loss with respect to our optimal parameter θ'_i and update our randomly initialized parameter θ:

$$\theta = \theta - \beta \nabla_\theta \sum_{T_i \sim p(T)} L_{T_i}(f_{\theta'_i})$$

Adversarial meta learning

We have seen how MAML is used to find the optimal parameter θ that is generalizable across tasks. Now, we will see a variant of MAML called ADML, which makes use of both clean and adversarial samples to find the better and robust initial model parameter θ. Before going ahead, let's understand what adversarial samples are. Adversarial samples are obtained as a result of adversarial attacks. Let's say we have an image; an adversarial attack consists of slightly modifying this image in such a way that it is not detectable to our eyes, and this modified image is called adversarial image. When we feed this adversarial image to the model, it fails to classify it correctly. There are several different adversarial attacks used to get the adversarial samples. We will see one of the commonly used methods called **Fast Gradient Sign Method (FGSM)**.

FGSM

Let's say we are performing an image classification; in general, we train the model by computing the loss and trying to minimize the loss by calculating gradients of our loss with respect to our model parameters, such as weights, and updating our model parameter. To get the adversarial sample of our image, we calculate the gradients of our loss with respect to the input pixels of our image, instead of the model parameter. So, the adversarial sample of an image is basically the gradient of loss with respect to the image. We take only one gradient step and so it is computationally effective. After calculating the gradients, we take the sign of it.

An adversarial image can be calculated as follows:

$$X_{adv} = x + \epsilon\, sign(\nabla_x J(x, y_{true}))$$

In the previous equation, the following applies:

- x_{adv} is the adversarial image
- x is the input image
- $\nabla_x J(x, y_{true})$ is the gradient of loss with respect to our input image

As you can see in the following diagram, we have an input image **x**, and we get the adversarial image by just adding the sign of gradient of our loss with respect to our image, to the actual image:

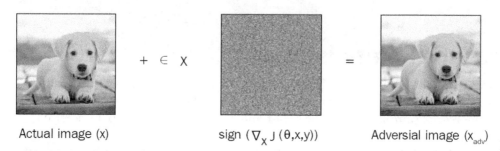

Actual image (x)   sign (∇_X J (θ,x,y))   Adversial image (x$_{adv}$)

ADML

Now that we have seen what adversarial samples are and how to generate adversarial samples, we will see how to use these adversarial samples in meta learning. We train our meta learning model with both clean samples and adversarial samples. But what is the need for training the model with adversarial samples? It helps us to find the robust model parameter θ. Both the clean and adversarial samples are used in the inner and outer loops of the algorithm and contribute equally to update the model parameter. ADML uses this varying correlation between clean and adversarial samples to obtain a better and robust initialization of model parameters so that our parameter becomes robust to adversarial samples and generalizes well to new tasks.

So, when we have a task distribution *p(T)*, we sample a batch of tasks T_i from the task distribution and, for each task, we sample *k* data points and prepare our train and test sets.

In ADML, we sample clean and adversarial samples for both train and test sets as $D^{train}_{clean_i}$, $D^{train}_{adv_i}$, $D^{test}_{clean_i}$, and $D^{test}_{adv_i}$.

Now we calculate loss on our train set, minimize the loss by gradient descent, and find the optimal parameter θ'. Since we have clean and adversarial training sets, we perform gradient descent on both of these sets and find the optimal parameter for both clean and adversarial sets as θ'_{clean_i} and θ'_{adv_i} respectively:

$$\theta'_{clean_i} = \theta - \alpha_1 \nabla_\theta L_{T_i}\left(f_\theta, D^{train}_{clean_i}\right)$$

$$\theta'_{adv_i} = \theta - \alpha_2 \nabla_\theta L_{T_i}\left(f_\theta, D^{train}_{adv_i}\right)$$

Now, we go to the meta training phase where we find the optimal parameter θ by minimizing loss on the test set by computing gradient of our loss with respect to optimal parameter θ' obtained in the previous step.

So, we update our model parameter θ by minimizing loss on both clean $D^{test}_{clean_i}$ and adversarial $D^{test}_{adv_i}$ test sets by computing gradient of loss with respect to an optimal parameter θ'_{clean_i} and θ'_{adv_i}:

$$\theta = \theta - \beta_1 \nabla_\theta \sum_{T_i \sim p(T)} L_{T_i}\left(f_{\theta'_{clean_i}}, D^{test}_{clean_i}\right)$$

$$\theta = \theta - \beta_2 \nabla_\theta \sum_{T_i \sim p(T)} L_{T_i}\left(f_{\theta'_{adv_i}}, D^{test}_{adv_i}\right)$$

Building ADML from scratch

In the last section, we saw how ADML works. We saw how we train our model with both clean and adversarial samples to obtain a better and robust model parameter θ that is generalizable across tasks. Now we will better understand ADML by coding them from scratch. For better understanding, we will consider a simple binary classification task. We randomly generate our input data and we train it with a single layer neural network and try to find the optimal parameter theta. Now, we will see step-by-step how exactly ADML works.

You can also check the code available as a Jupyter Notebook with an explanation here: https://github.com/sudharsan13296/Hands-On-Meta-Learning-With-Python/blob/master/06.%20MAML%20and%20it's%20Variants/6.7%20Building%20ADML%20From%20Scratch.ipynb.

First, we import all of the necessary libraries:

```
import tensorflow as tf
import numpy as np
```

Generating data points

Now, we define a function called `sample_points` for generating clean input (x, y) pairs. It takes the k parameter as input, which implies a number of (x, y) pairs we want to sample:

```
def sample_points(k):
    x = np.random.rand(k,50)
    y = np.random.choice([0, 1], size=k, p=[.5, .5]).reshape([-1,1])
    return x,y
```

The preceding function returns the following output:

```
x, y = sample_points(10)
print x[0]
print y[0]

[0.69922136 0.77305793 0.72227583 0.45291578 0.52828294 0.65308614
 0.77281836 0.59878078 0.71554901 0.51660327 0.65538137 0.25267594
 0.13763862 0.12522582 0.16336571 0.87987815 0.64465771 0.86281232
 0.24503599 0.85324859 0.62247917 0.58166159 0.47871545 0.75025566
 0.87919612 0.49545388 0.31058753 0.66306459 0.34621453 0.56970739
 0.84310111 0.08747573 0.48944231 0.50061581 0.86215915 0.3248433
 0.01350084 0.23846395 0.91015074 0.04968178 0.59098773 0.74692099
 0.92763503 0.16319537 0.69655162 0.20419323 0.58241944 0.15703596
 0.76047838 0.93452557]
[0]
```

FGSM

Now, we define one more function called `FGSM` for generating adversarial inputs. We use FGSM for generating adversarial samples. We have seen how FGSM generates the adversarial pairs by calculating gradients with respect to the input instead of the model parameter. So, we take clean (x, y) pairs as input and generate adversarial (x_adv, y) pairs:

```
def FGSM(x,y):

    #placeholder for the inputs x and y
    X = tf.placeholder(tf.float32)
    Y = tf.placeholder(tf.float32)

    #initialize theta with random values
    theta = tf.Variable(tf.zeros([50,1]))

    #predict the value of y
    YHat = tf.nn.softmax(tf.matmul(X, theta))

    #calculate the loss
    loss = tf.reduce_mean(-tf.reduce_sum(Y*tf.log(YHat),
reduction_indices=1))

    #now calculate gradient of our loss function with respect to our input
X instead of model parameter theta
    gradient = ((tf.gradients(loss,X)[0]))
    #calculate the adversarial input
    #i.e x_adv = x + epsilon * sign ( nabla_x J(X, Y))
    X_adv = X + 0.2*tf.sign(gradient)
    X_adv = tf.clip_by_value(X_adv,-1.0,1.0)

    #start the tensoflow session
    with tf.Session() as sess:

        sess.run(tf.global_variables_initializer())
        X_adv = sess.run(X_adv, feed_dict={X: x, Y: y})
    return X_adv, y
```

Single layer neural network

We use a neural network with a single layer for predicting the output:

```
a = np.matmul(X, theta)
 YHat = sigmoid(a)
```

So, we use ADML for finding this optimal parameter value θ that is generalizable across tasks. So, for a new task, we can learn from a few data points in less time by taking fewer gradient steps.

Adversarial meta learning

Now, we define a class called ADML where we implement the ADML algorithm. In the __init__ method, we will initialize all of the necessary variables. Then, we define our sigmoid function and we define our train function.

We will see this step-by-step and later see the final code as a whole:

```
class ADML(object):
```

We define the __init__ method and initialize necessary variables:

```
    def __init__(self):
```

We initialize a number of tasks—that is, the number of tasks we need in each batch of tasks:

```
        self.num_tasks = 2
```

We initialize a number of samples—that is, a number of shots—a number of data points (k) we need to have in each task:

```
        self.num_samples = 10
```

We initialize a number of epochs—that is, training iterations:

```
        self.epochs = 100
```

The hyperparameter for the inner loop (inner gradient update) is as follows:

```
        #for clean sample

        self.alpha1 = 0.0001

        #for adversarial sample

        self.alpha2 = 0.0001
```

The hyperparameter for the outer loop (outer gradient update), which is meta optimization, is as follows:

```
#for clean sample
self.beta1 = 0.0001
#for adversarial sample
self.beta2 = 0.0001
```

We randomly initialize our model parameter, `theta`:

```
self.theta = np.random.normal(size=50).reshape(50, 1)
```

We define our `sigmoid` activation function:

```
def sigmoid(self,a):
    return 1.0 / (1 + np.exp(-a))
```

Now, let's see how to train the network:

```
def train(self):
```

For the number of epochs:

```
for e in range(self.epochs):

    #theta' of clean samples
    self.theta_clean = []

    #theta' of adversarial samples
    self.theta_adv = []
```

For task `i` in batch of tasks:

```
for i in range(self.num_tasks):
```

We sample k data points and prepare our training data. First, we sample the clean data points, that is, $D^{train}_{clean_i}$:

```
XTrain_clean, YTrain_clean =
sample_points(self.num_samples)
```

Feed the clean samples to FGSM and get adversarial samples $D^{train}_{adv_i}$:

```
XTrain_adv, YTrain_adv = FGSM(XTrain_clean,YTrain_clean)
```

Now, we compute θ'_{clean_i} and store it in `theta_clean`. Predict the output y using the single layer network:

```
a = np.matmul(XTrain_clean, self.theta)

YHat = self.sigmoid(a)
```

Since we are performing classification, we use cross entropy loss as our loss function:

```
loss = ((np.matmul(-YTrain_clean.T, np.log(YHat)) -
np.matmul((1 -YTrain_clean.T), np.log(1 - YHat)))/self.num_samples)[0][0]
```

We minimize the loss by calculating the gradients:

```
gradient = np.matmul(XTrain_clean.T, (YHat - YTrain_clean))
/ self.num_samples
```

We update the gradients and find the optimal parameter θ'_{clean_i} for clean samples, $\theta'_{clean_i} = \theta - \alpha_1 \nabla_\theta L_{T_i}(f_\theta, D^{train}_{clean_i})$:

```
self.theta_clean.append(self.theta - self.alpha1*gradient)
```

Now, we compute θ'_{adv_i} for adversarial samples and store it in `theta_adv`:

```
#predict the output y
a = (np.matmul(XTrain_adv, self.theta))

YHat = self.sigmoid(a)

#calculate cross entropy loss
loss = ((np.matmul(-YTrain_adv.T, np.log(YHat)) -
np.matmul((1 -YTrain_adv.T), np.log(1 - YHat)))/self.num_samples)[0][0]
#minimize the loss by calculating gradients
gradient = np.matmul(XTrain_adv.T, (YHat - YTrain_adv)) /
self.num_samples
```

We update the gradients and find the optimal parameter θ'_{adv_i} for adversarial samples,

$\theta'_{adv_i} = \theta - \alpha_2 \nabla_\theta L_{T_i}(f_\theta, D^{train}_{adv_i})$:

```
self.theta_adv.append(self.theta - self.alpha2*gradient)
```

We initialize meta gradients for clean samples and adversarial samples:

```
meta_gradient_clean = np.zeros(self.theta.shape)

#initialize meta gradients for adversarial samples
meta_gradient_adv = np.zeros(self.theta.shape)
```

For `i` in number of tasks:

```
for i in range(self.num_tasks):
```

We sample k data points and prepare our clean and adversarial test sets (meta-train sets) for meta training—that is, $D_{clean_i}^{test}$ and $D_{adv_i}^{test}$:

```
#first, we sample clean data points
XTest_clean, YTest_clean = sample_points(self.num_samples)

#feed the clean samples to FGSM and get adversarial samples
XTest_adv, YTest_adv = sample_points(self.num_samples)
```

First, we compute meta gradients for clean samples:

```
#predict the value of y
a = np.matmul(XTest_clean, self.theta_clean[i])
YPred = self.sigmoid(a)
#compute meta gradients
meta_gradient_clean += np.matmul(XTest_clean.T, (YPred -
YTest_clean)) / self.num_samples
```

Now, we compute meta gradients for adversarial samples:

```
#predict the value of y
a = (np.matmul(XTest_adv, self.theta_adv[i]))
YPred = self.sigmoid(a)
#compute meta gradients
meta_gradient_adv += np.matmul(XTest_adv.T, (YPred -
YTest_adv)) / self.num_samples
```

We update our randomly initialized model parameter θ with the meta gradients of both clean and adversarial samples:

$$\theta = \theta - \beta_1 \nabla_\theta \sum_{T_i \sim p(T)} L_{T_i}\left(f_{\theta'_{clean_i}}, D^{test}_{clean_i}\right)$$

$$\theta = \theta - \beta_2 \nabla_\theta \sum_{T_i \sim p(T)} L_{T_i}\left(f_{\theta'_{adv_i}}, D^{test}_{adv_i}\right)$$

```
        self.theta = self.theta-
self.beta1*meta_gradient_clean/self.num_tasks
```

```
        self.theta = self.theta-
self.beta2*meta_gradient_adv/self.num_tasks
```

We print the loss for every 10 epochs:

```
        if e%10==0:
            print "Epoch {}: Loss {}\n".format(e,loss)
            print 'Updated Model Parameter Theta\n'
            print 'Sampling Next Batch of Tasks \n'
            print '---------------------------------\n'
```

The whole code for `ADML` class is as follows:

```
class ADML(object):
    def __init__(self):

        #initialize number of tasks i.e number of tasks we need in each
batch of tasks
        self.num_tasks = 2
        #number of samples i.e number of shots -number of data points (k)
we need to have in each task
        self.num_samples = 10

        #number of epochs i.e training iterations
        self.epochs = 100
        #hyperparameter for the inner loop (inner gradient update)

        #for clean sample
        self.alpha1 = 0.0001

        #for adversarial sample
        self.alpha2 = 0.0001
        #hyperparameter for the outer loop (outer gradient update) i.e meta
optimization
```

```
YTest_adv)) / self.num_samples

        #update our randomly initialized model parameter theta
        #with the meta gradients of both clean and adversarial samples
        self.theta = self.theta-
self.beta1*meta_gradient_clean/self.num_tasks

        self.theta = self.theta-
self.beta2*meta_gradient_adv/self.num_tasks
        if e%10==0:
            print "Epoch {}: Loss {}\n".format(e,loss)
            print 'Updated Model Parameter Theta\n'
            print 'Sampling Next Batch of Tasks \n'
            print '-------------------------------\n'
```

We create an instance to our ADML class:

```
model = ADML()
```

Then, we start training the model:

```
model.train()
```

You can notice how the loss is decreasing over epochs:

```
Epoch 0: Loss 100.25943711532

Updated Model Parameter Theta

Sampling Next Batch of Tasks

-------------------------------

Epoch 10: Loss 2.13533264312

Updated Model Parameter Theta

Sampling Next Batch of Tasks

-------------------------------

Epoch 20: Loss 0.426824910313

Updated Model Parameter Theta

Sampling Next Batch of Tasks
```

CAML

We have seen how MAML finds the optimal initial parameter of a model so that it can easily be adaptable to a new task with fewer gradient steps. Now, we will see an interesting variant of MAML called CAML. The idea of CAML is very simple, same as MAML; it also tries to find the better initial parameter. We learned how MAML uses two loops; on the inner loop, MAML learns the parameter specific to the task and tries to minimize the loss using gradient descent and, on the outer loop, it updates the model parameter to reduce the expected loss across several tasks so that we can use the updated model parameter as better initializations for related tasks.

In CAML, we perform a very small tweak to the MAML algorithm. Here, instead of using a single model parameter, we split our model parameter into two:

- **Context parameter**: It is task-specific parameter updated on the inner loop. It is denoted by $\emptyset$ and it is specific to each task and represents the embeddings of an individual task.
- **Shared parameter**: It is shared across tasks and updated in the outer loop to find the optimal model parameter. It is denoted by θ.

So, the context parameter is adapted in the inner loop for each task and the shared parameter is shared across tasks and used for meta training in an outer loop. We initialize the context parameter to zero before each adaptation step.

Okay; but what is really useful in splitting our parameter into two different parameters? It is used to avoid overfitting with respect to particular tasks, promotes faster learning, and it is memory efficient.

CAML algorithm

Now, let's see how CAML works steps by step:

1. Let's say we have a model f parameterized by a parameter θ and we have a distribution over tasks $p(T)$. First, we randomly initialize the model parameter θ. We also initialize our context parameter $\emptyset_0 = 0$.
2. Now, we sample some batch of tasks T_i from a distribution of tasks, that is, $T_i \sim p(T)$.

3. **Inner loop**: For each task (T_i) in tasks (T), we sample k data points and prepare our train and test datasets:

$$D_i^{train} = \{(x_1, y_1), (x_2, y_2), \ldots (x_k, y_k)\}$$

$$D_i^{test} = \{(x_1, y_1), (x_2, y_2), \ldots (x_k, y_k)\}$$

Now, we set our context parameter to 0:

$$\phi_0 = 0$$

Then, we calculate loss on D_i^{train}, minimize the loss using gradient descent, and learn the task specific parameter $\varnothing_i$:

$$\phi_i = \phi_0 - \alpha \nabla_\phi L_{Ti}(f_{\phi_0, \theta})$$

4. **Outer loop**: Now, we perform meta optimization in the test set—that is, here we try to minimize the loss in the test set D_i^{test} and find the optimal parameter:

$$\theta = \theta - \beta \nabla_\phi \sum_{T_i \sim p(T)} L_{Ti}(f_{\phi_i, \theta})$$

5. Repeat steps 2 to step 4 for n number of iterations.

Summary

In this chapter, we have learned how to find the optimal model parameter θ that is generalizable across tasks so that we can take fewer gradient steps and learn quickly on the new related tasks. We started off with MAML and we saw how MAML performs meta optimization to calculate the optimal model parameter. Next, we saw adversarial meta learning where we used both clean and adversarial samples for finding the robust initial model parameter. Later, we learned about CAML and we saw how it uses two different parameters, one for learning within the task and one for updating the model parameter.

In the next chapter, we will learn about meta-SGD and Reptile algorithm, which is again used for finding the better initial parameter of a model.

Questions

1. What is MAML?
2. Why is MAML model agnostic?
3. What is adversarial meta learning?
4. What is FGSM?
5. What is the context parameter?
6. What is the shared parameter?

Further reading

- MAML paper: https://arxiv.org/pdf/1703.03400.pdf
- Adversarial meta learning paper: https://arxiv.org/pdf/1806.03316.pdf
- CAML paper: https://arxiv.org/pdf/1810.03642.pdf

7
Meta-SGD and Reptile

In the last chapter, we learned how MAML is used for finding an optimal parameter that's generalizable across several tasks. We saw how MAML computes this optimal parameter by calculating meta gradients and performing meta optimization. We also saw adversarial meta learning, which acts as an enhancement to MAML by adding adversarial samples and allowing MAML to wrestle between clean and adversarial samples to find the optimal parameter. We also saw CAML—or, context adaptation for meta learning. In this chapter, we'll learn about Meta-SGD, another meta learning algorithm that's used for performing learning quickly. Unlike MAML, Meta-SGD will not just find the optimal parameter, it will also find the optimal learning rate and an update direction. We'll see how to use Meta-SGD in supervised and reinforcement learning settings. We'll also see how to build Meta-SGD from scratch. Going ahead, we'll learn about the Reptile algorithm, which acts an improvement to MAML. We'll see how Reptile differs from MAML and then we'll cover how to use Reptile in sine wave regression tasks.

In this chapter, you'll learn about the following:

- Meta-SGD
- Meta-SGD in supervised learning
- Meta-SGD in reinforcement learning
- Building Meta-SGD from scratch
- Reptile
- Sine wave regression using Reptile

Meta-SGD

Let's say we have some task, T. We use a model, f, parameterized by some parameter, θ, and train the model to minimize the loss. We minimize the loss using gradient descent and find the optimal parameter θ for the model.

Let's recall the update rule of a gradient descent:

$$\theta = \theta - \alpha \nabla_\theta L_{T_i}(f_\theta)$$

So, what are the key elements that make up our gradient descent? Let's see:

- Parameter θ
- Learning rate α
- Update direction

We usually set the parameter θ to some random value and try to find the optimal value during our training process, and we set the value of learning rate α to a small number or decay it over time and an update direction that follows the gradient. Can we learn all of these key elements of the gradient descent by meta learning so that we can learn quickly from a few data points? We've already seen, in the last chapter, how MAML finds the optimal initial parameter θ that's generalizable across tasks. With the optimal initial parameter, we can take fewer gradient steps and learn quickly on a new task.

So, now can we learn the optimal learning rate and update direction that're generalizable across tasks so we can achieve faster convergence and training? Let's see how we can learn this in Meta-SGD by comparing it with MAML. If you recall, in the MAML inner loop, find the optimal parameter θ'_i for each task T_i by minimizing the loss through gradient descent:

$$\theta'_i = \theta - \alpha \nabla_\theta L_{T_i}(f_\theta)$$

For Meta-SGD, we can rewrite the previous equation as follows:

$$\theta'_i = \theta - \alpha \circ \nabla_\theta L_{T_i}(f_\theta)$$

But what's the difference? Here α is not just a scalar small value but a vector. We initialize α randomly with same shape as θ. We call θ as an initial parameter and $\alpha \circ \nabla_\theta L_{T_i}(f_\theta)$ as an adaptation term. So, the adaptation term $\alpha \circ \nabla_\theta L_{T_i}(f_\theta)$ represents the update direction and its length becomes the learning rate. We update our values in the $\alpha \circ \nabla_\theta L_{T_i}(f_\theta)$ direction instead of the gradient direction, $\nabla_\theta L_{T_i}(f_\theta)$, and our learning rate is implicitly implemented in the adaptation term.

So, in Meta-SGD, we don't initialize a learning rate α with some small scalar value. Instead, we initialize the learning rate with random values with the same shape as θ and learn them along with θ. We sample some batch of tasks and, for each task, we sample some k data points and minimize the loss using gradient descent, but our update equation becomes the following:

$$\theta'_i = \theta - \alpha \circ \nabla_\theta L_{T_i}(f_\theta)$$

That is, our update direction is the adaptation term direction and not the gradient direction, and we learn α along with θ.

Now, in the outer loop, we perform meta optimization—that is, we calculate gradients of loss with respect to optimal parameters θ'_i and update our randomly initialized model parameter θ. In Meta-SGD, instead of updating θ alone, we also update our randomly initialized α, as follows:

$$\theta = \theta - \beta \nabla_\theta \sum_{T_i \sim p(T)} L_{T_i}(f_{\theta'_i})$$

$$\alpha = \alpha - \beta \nabla_\alpha \sum_{T_i \sim p(T)} L_{T_i}(f_{\theta'_i})$$

As you can see, Meta-SGD is just a small tweak over MAML. In MAML, we randomly initialize the model parameter θ and try to find the optimal parameter that's generalizable across tasks. In Meta-SGD, instead of just learning the model parameter θ, we also learn the learning rate and update direction, which is implicitly implemented in the adaptation term.

Meta-SGD for supervised learning

Now, we'll see how to use Meta-SGD in a supervised learning setting. Like MAML, we can apply Meta-SGD to any of the supervised learning problems, be it regression or classification, that can be trained with gradient descent. First, we need to define the loss function we wish to use. For example, if we're performing classification, we can use cross-entropy as our loss function and, if we're performing regression, we can use mean squared error as our loss function. We can use any loss function suitable for our tasks. Let's go through this step-by-step:

1. Let's say we have a model f parameterized by a parameter θ and we have a distribution over tasks $p(T)$. First, we randomly initialize the model parameter θ and we randomly initialize α with the same shape as θ.

2. We sample some batch of tasks T_i from a distribution of tasks: $T_i \sim p(T)$. Let's say we have sampled three tasks, then $T = \{T_1, T_2, T_3\}$.

3. **Inner loop**: For each task (T_i) in tasks (T), we sample k data points and prepare our train and test datasets:

$$D_i^{train} = \{(x_1, y_1), (x_2, y_2). \dots \dots (x_k, y_k)\}$$

$$D_i^{test} = \{(x_1, y_1), (x_2, y_2). \dots \dots (x_k, y_k)\}$$

Now we apply some supervised learning algorithm on D_i^{train}, calculate and minimize the loss using gradient descent and get the optimal parameters θ_i':
$\theta_i' = \theta - \alpha \circ \nabla_\theta L_{T_i}(f_\theta)$.

So, for each of the tasks, we sample k data points and minimize the loss on the train set D_i^{train} and get the optimal parameters θ_i'. As we sampled three tasks, we'll have three optimal parameters $\{\theta_1', \theta_2', \theta_3'\}$.

4. **Outer loop**: Now, we perform meta optimization in the test set(meta-train set)—that is, here we try to minimize the loss in the test set D_i^{test}. We minimize the loss by calculating the gradient with respect to our optimal parameter θ_i' calculated in the previous step, and update our randomly initialized parameter θ using our test set. We not only update θ, we also update our randomly initialized parameter α and it can be expressed as follows:

$$\theta = \theta - \beta \nabla_\theta \sum_{T_i \sim p(T)} L_{T_i}(f_{\theta_i'})$$

$$\alpha = \alpha - \beta \nabla_\theta \sum_{T_i \sim p(T)} L_{T_i}(f_{\theta_i'})$$

5. We repeat steps 2 to step 4 for n number of iterations.

Building Meta-SGD from scratch

In the last section, we saw how Meta-SGD works. We saw how Meta-SGD obtains a better and robust model parameter θ that's generalizable across tasks along with optimal learning rate and update direction. Now, we'll better understand Meta-SGD by coding them from scratch. Like we did in MAML, for better understanding, we'll consider a simple binary classification task. We randomly generate our input data and we train it with a simple single layer neural network and try to find the optimal parameter θ. We'll see step-by-step exactly how to do this.

You can also check the code available as a Jupyter Notebook with an explanation here: `https://github.com/sudharsan13296/Hands-On-Meta-Learning-With-Python/blob/master/07.%20Meta-SGD%20and%20Reptile%20Algorithms/7.4%20Building%20Meta-SGD%20from%20Scratch.ipynb`.

First, we import the `numpy` library:

```
import numpy as np
```

Generating data points

Now, we define a function called `sample_points` for generating our input (x, y) pairs. It takes the parameter k as input, which implies the number of (x, y) pairs we want to sample:

```
def sample_points(k):
    x = np.random.rand(k,50)
    y = np.random.choice([0, 1], size=k, p=[.5, .5]).reshape([-1,1])
    return x,y
```

The preceding function returns output as follows:

```
x, y = sample_points(10)
print x[0]
print y[0]

[5.01913307e-01 1.01874941e-01 7.16678998e-01 3.90294047e-01
 2.95330904e-01 8.66751993e-01 5.09988127e-01 8.59389493e-01
 5.16202142e-01 7.92016358e-01 8.24237307e-01 7.76739141e-01
 8.57034917e-01 2.75862141e-01 6.44874856e-01 2.75248940e-01
 5.67665047e-01 9.61564994e-01 7.58931873e-01 1.08989614e-02
 7.69325529e-01 4.05955016e-01 1.98799935e-01 9.94134622e-01
 3.07179216e-01 1.34756367e-01 2.92326855e-01 5.00026528e-01
 7.23673231e-01 5.28698231e-01 1.52495715e-01 9.20139339e-01
 1.76127500e-02 2.42244262e-01 7.09515862e-01 7.10358091e-01
 6.47656449e-01 5.15623266e-01 8.77002211e-01 4.18744855e-01
 9.67902538e-01 8.79261670e-01 5.88524781e-01 5.11397703e-02
```

```
7.07513737e-01 4.61998029e-01 8.77306226e-01 5.32049083e-01
8.07178697e-01 5.01521846e-04]
[1]
```

Single layer neural network

We use a neural network with only a single layer for predicting the output:

```
a = np.matmul(X, theta)
YHat = sigmoid(a)
```

So, we use Meta-SGD for finding this optimal parameter value theta, and learning rate and gradient update direction that's generalizable across tasks. So, for a new task, we can learn from a few data points in less time by taking fewer gradient steps.

Meta-SGD

Now, we define a class called `MetaSGD` where we implement the Meta-SGD algorithm. In the __init__ method, we'll initialize all the necessary variables. Then, we define our sigmoid activation function. After this, we define our train function:

```
class MetaSGD(object):
```

We define the __init__ method and initialize all necessary variables:

```
    def __init__(self):
        #initialize number of tasks i.e number of tasks we need in each
batch of tasks
        self.num_tasks = 2
        #number of samples i.e number of shots -number of data points (k)
we need to have in each task
        self.num_samples = 10

        #number of epochs i.e training iterations
        self.epochs = 10000
        #hyperparameter for the outer loop (outer gradient update) i.e meta
optimization
        self.beta = 0.0001
        #randomly initialize our model parameter theta
        self.theta = np.random.normal(size=50).reshape(50, 1)
        #randomly initialize alpha with same shape as theta
        self.alpha = np.random.normal(size=50).reshape(50, 1)
```

We define our `sigmoid` activation function:

```
    def sigmoid(self,a):
        return 1.0 / (1 + np.exp(-a))
```

Now, let's start training:

```
def train(self):
```

For the number of epochs:

```
for e in range(self.epochs):

    self.theta_ = []
```

For the `i` task in a batch of tasks:

```
for i in range(self.num_tasks):
```

We sample *k* data points and prepare our train set:

```
XTrain, YTrain = sample_points(self.num_samples)
```

Then, we predict the value of *y* using a single layer network:

```
a = np.matmul(XTrain, self.theta)

YHat = self.sigmoid(a)
```

We compute the loss and calculate gradients:

```
        #since we're performing classification, we use cross
    entropy loss as our loss function
        loss = ((np.matmul(-YTrain.T, np.log(YHat)) - np.matmul((1
    -YTrain.T), np.log(1 - YHat)))/self.num_samples)[0][0]
            #minimize the loss by calculating gradients
            gradient = np.matmul(XTrain.T, (YHat - YTrain)) /
    self.num_samples
```

After that, we update the gradients and find the optimal parameter θ' for each of the tasks:

```
        self.theta_.append(self.theta -
    (np.multiply(self.alpha,gradient)))
```

We initialize the meta gradients:

```
meta_gradient = np.zeros(self.theta.shape)

for i in range(self.num_tasks):
```

We sample k data points and prepare our test set for meta training D_i^{test}:

```
XTest, YTest = sample_points(10)
```

We then predict the value of y:

```
a = np.matmul(XTest, self.theta_[i])
YPred = self.sigmoid(a)
```

We compute the meta gradients:

```
meta_gradient += np.matmul(XTest.T, (YPred - YTest)) /
self.num_samples
```

Now, we update our model parameter, `theta`, and `alpha`:

$$\theta = \theta - \beta \nabla_\theta \sum_{T_i \sim p(T)} L_{T_i}\left(f_{\theta_i'}\right)$$

$$\alpha = \alpha - \beta \nabla_\theta \sum_{T_i \sim p(T)} L_{T_i}\left(f_{\theta_i'}\right)$$

```
self.theta = self.theta-self.beta*meta_gradient/self.num_tasks
self.alpha = self.alpha-self.beta*meta_gradient/self.num_tasks
```

We print the loss for every 1,000 epochs:

```
if e%1000==0:
    print "Epoch {}: Loss {}\n".format(e,loss)
    print 'Updated Model Parameter Theta\n'
    print 'Sampling Next Batch of Tasks \n'
    print '---------------------------------\n'
```

The complete code for `MetaSGD` is given as follows:

```
class MetaSGD(object):
    def __init__(self):
        #initialize number of tasks i.e number of tasks we need in each
batch of tasks
        self.num_tasks = 2
        #number of samples i.e number of shots -number of data points (k)
we need to have in each task
        self.num_samples = 10

        #number of epochs i.e training iterations
        self.epochs = 10000
        #hyperparameter for the inner loop (inner gradient update)
```

```
        self.alpha = 0.0001
        #hyperparameter for the outer loop (outer gradient update) i.e meta
optimization
        self.beta = 0.0001
        #randomly initialize our model parameter theta
        self.theta = np.random.normal(size=50).reshape(50, 1)
        #randomly initialize alpha with same shape as theta
        self.alpha = np.random.normal(size=50).reshape(50, 1)
    #define our sigmoid activation function
    def sigmoid(self,a):
        return 1.0 / (1 + np.exp(-a))
    #now let's get to the interesting part i.e training :P
    def train(self):
        #for the number of epochs,
        for e in range(self.epochs):
            self.theta_ = []
            #for task i in batch of tasks
            for i in range(self.num_tasks):
                #sample k data points and prepare our train set
                XTrain, YTrain = sample_points(self.num_samples)
                a = np.matmul(XTrain, self.theta)

                YHat = self.sigmoid(a)

                #since we're performing classification, we use cross
entropy loss as our loss function
                loss = ((np.matmul(-YTrain.T, np.log(YHat)) - np.matmul((1
-YTrain.T), np.log(1 - YHat)))/self.num_samples)[0][0]
                #minimize the loss by calculating gradients
                gradient = np.matmul(XTrain.T, (YHat - YTrain)) /
self.num_samples

                #update the gradients and find the optimal parameter theta'
for each of tasks
                self.theta_.append(self.theta -
(np.multiply(self.alpha,gradient)))
            #initialize meta gradients
            meta_gradient = np.zeros(self.theta.shape)
            for i in range(self.num_tasks):
                #sample k data points and prepare our test set for meta
training
                XTest, YTest = sample_points(10)

                #predict the value of y
                a = np.matmul(XTest, self.theta_[i])
                YPred = self.sigmoid(a)
                #compute meta gradients
                meta_gradient += np.matmul(XTest.T, (YPred - YTest)) /
```

```
        self.num_samples

                #update our randomly initialized model parameter theta with the
meta gradients
                self.theta = self.theta-self.beta*meta_gradient/self.num_tasks
                #update our randomly initialized hyperparameter alpha with the
meta gradients
                self.alpha = self.alpha-self.beta*meta_gradient/self.num_tasks
                if e%1000==0:
                    print "Epoch {}: Loss {}\n".format(e,loss)
                    print 'Updated Model Parameter Theta\n'
                    print 'Sampling Next Batch of Tasks \n'
                    print '-------------------------------\n'
```

We create an instance of our `MetaSGD` class:

```
model = MetaSGD()
```

Let's start training the model:

```
model.train()
```

You can see how the loss minimizes through various epochs:

```
Epoch 0: Loss 2.22523195333

Updated Model Parameter Theta

Sampling Next Batch of Tasks

-------------------------------

Epoch 1000: Loss 1.951785305709

Updated Model Parameter Theta

Sampling Next Batch of Tasks

-------------------------------

Epoch 2000: Loss 1.47382270343

Updated Model Parameter Theta

Sampling Next Batch of Tasks

-------------------------------
```

```
Epoch 3000: Loss 1.07296354822

Updated Model Parameter Theta

Sampling Next Batch of Tasks

-----------------------------------
```

Meta-SGD for reinforcement learning

Now we'll see how to use Meta-SGD in reinforcement learning. Meta-SGD is compatible with any RL algorithm that can be trained with gradient descent.

1. Let's say we have a model f parameterized by a parameter θ and we have a distribution over tasks $p(T)$. First, we randomly initialize the model parameter θ and we randomly initialize α whose shape is the same as θ.

2. Sample some batch of tasks T_i from a distribution of tasks: $T_i \sim p(T)$. Say, we have sampled three tasks, $T = \{T_1, T_2, T_3\}$.

3. **Inner loop**: For each task (T_i) in tasks (T), we sample D_i^{train} trajectories, calculate the loss and minimize the loss using gradient descent and get the optimal parameters θ_i': $\theta_i' = \theta - \alpha \circ \nabla_\theta L_{T_i}(f_\theta)$. So for each of the tasks, we sample trajectories, minimize the loss and get the optimal parameters θ_i'. As we sampled three tasks, we'll have three optimal parameters $\{\theta_1', \theta_2', \theta_3'\}$ for all of the three tasks. Next, we'll sample another set of trajectories called D_i^{test} for meta update.

4. **Outer loop**: Now, we perform meta optimization in the D_i^{test} trajectory. We minimize the loss by calculating the gradient with respect to our optimal parameter θ_i' obtained in the previous step, update our randomly initialized parameter θ and α:

$$\theta = \theta - \beta \nabla_\theta \sum_{T_i \sim p(T)} L_{T_i}(f_{\theta_i'})$$

$$\alpha = \alpha - \beta \nabla_\theta \sum_{T_i \sim p(T)} L_{T_i}(f_{\theta_i'})$$

5. We repeat steps 2 to step 4 for n number of iterations.

Reptile

The Reptile algorithm has been proposed as an improvement to MAML by OpenAI. It's simple and easier to implement. We know that, in MAML, we calculate second order derivatives—that is, the gradient of gradients. But computationally, this isn't an efficient task. So, OpenAI came up with an improvement over MAML called Reptile. The algorithm of Reptile is very simple. Sample some n number of tasks and run **Stochastic Gradient Descent (SGD)** for fewer iterations on each of the sampled tasks and then update our model parameter in a direction that's common to all of the tasks. Since we're performing SGD for fewer iterations on each task, it indirectly implies we're calculating the second order derivative over the loss. Unlike MAML, it's computationally effective as we're not calculating the second order derivative directly nor unrolling the computational graph, and so it is easier to implement.

Let's say we sampled two tasks, T_1 and T_2, from the task distribution and we randomly initialize the model parameter θ. First, we take task T_1 and perform SGD for some n iterations and get the optimal parameter θ_1'. Then we take next task T_2, perform SGD for n iterations and get the optimal parameter θ_2'. So, we have two optimal sets of parameters: $\theta' = \{\theta_1', \theta_2'\}$. Now we need to move our parameter θ in a direction that's closer to both of these optimal parameters as shown in the following diagram:

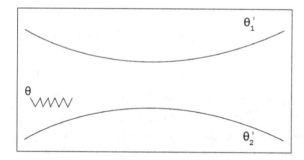

But how can we move our randomly initialized model parameter θ in a direction closer to the optimal parameter θ'? First, we need to find the distance between our randomly initialized model parameter θ and optimal set of parameters θ'. So we use Euclidean distance D as our distance measure for finding this distance. Once we find the distance between θ and θ', we need to minimize them:

$$Minimize_\theta \mathbb{E}[\frac{1}{2}D(\theta, \theta')^2]$$

Minimizing the distance between θ and θ' essentially moves our randomly initialized model parameter θ in a direction closer to the optimal parameter θ'. But how can we minimize this distance? We basically compute gradients of the distance $\nabla_\theta \mathbb{E}[\frac{1}{2}D(\theta,\theta')^2]$ for minimizing and it can be written as follows:

$$\theta = \theta - \epsilon \nabla_\theta \mathbb{E}[\frac{1}{2}D(\theta,\theta')^2]$$

So, after calculating gradients, our final update equation becomes the following:

$$\theta = \theta + \epsilon(\theta' - \theta)$$

By updating our model parameter θ using the previous equation, we essentially minimize the distance between the initial parameter θ and optimal parameter values θ'. So, we find the optimal parameter for each task by performing SGD for n number of iterations. Once we get this optimal set of parameters, we update our model parameter θ using the previous equation.

The Reptile algorithm

Reptile is a simple yet effective algorithm. Reptile can be implemented in both serial and batch versions. In the serial version, we sample only one task from the task distribution while, in the batch version, we sample a batch of tasks and try to find the optimal parameter. We'll see how the serial version of Reptile works. The sequence of steps involved in Reptile is as follows:

1. Let's say we have a distribution over tasks $p(T)$, and we randomly initialize the model parameter θ.
2. Now we sample a task T from the task distribution: $T \sim p(T)$.
3. For the sampled task T, we sample some k data points and prepare our dataset D: $D = \{(x_1, y_1), (x_2, y_2)..... (x_k, y_k)\}$. Our dataset basically contains x features and y labels. Now, we minimize the loss in our dataset by performing stochastic gradient descent for some n number of iterations. After performing SGD for n number of iterations on our sampled task T, we'll get the optimal parameter θ'.
4. We update our randomly initialized parameter θ in a direction closer to the optimal parameter θ' obtained in previous steps as follows: $\theta = \theta + \epsilon(\theta' - \theta)$.
5. We repeat the steps 2 to step 4 for n number of iterations.

Sine wave regression using Reptile

In the last section, we saw how Reptile works. Now, we'll understand Reptile better by coding it from scratch. Let's say we have a collection of tasks and the goal of each task is to regress the output of the sine wave given some input. So what do we mean by that?

Let's say *y = amplitude*sin(x+phase)*. The goal of our algorithm is to learn to regress the value of *y* given *x*. The value of amplitude is chosen randomly between 0.1 and 5.0 and the value of phase is chosen randomly between 0 and π. So, for each of the tasks, we sample only 10 data points and train the network—that is, for each of the tasks, we sample only 10 *(x,y)* pairs. Let's get to the code and see it in detail.

You can also check the code available as a Jupyter Notebook with an explanation here:
`https://github.com/sudharsan13296/Hands-On-Meta-Learning-With-Python/blob/master/07.%20Meta-SGD%20and%20Reptile%20Algorithms/7.7%20Sine%20wave%20Regression%20Using%20Reptile.ipynb`.

First, we import all of the necessary libraries:

```
import tensorflow as tf
import numpy as np
```

Generating data points

Now we define a function called `sample_points` for generating *(x,y)* pairs. It takes the parameter k as input, which implies the number of *(x,y)* pairs we want to sample:

```
def sample_points(k):
    num_points = 100
    #amplitude
    amplitude = np.random.uniform(low=0.1, high=5.0)
    #phase
    phase = np.random.uniform(low=0, high=np.pi)

    x = np.linspace(-5, 5, num_points)

    #y = a*sin(x+b)
    y = amplitude * np.sin(x + phase)
    #sample k data points
    sample = np.random.choice(np.arange(num_points), size=k)
    return (x[sample], y[sample])
```

Two-layered neural network

Like MAML, Reptile is also compatible with any algorithms that can be trained with gradient descent. So, we use a simple two-layered neural network with 64 hidden units.

First, let's reset the TensorFlow graph:

```
tf.reset_default_graph()
```

We initialize the network parameters:

```
num_hidden = 64
num_classes = 1
num_feature = 1
```

Next, we define the placeholders for our input and output:

```
X = tf.placeholder(tf.float32, shape=[None, num_feature])
Y = tf.placeholder(tf.float32, shape=[None, num_classes])
```

We randomly initialize our model parameters:

```
w1 = tf.Variable(tf.random_uniform([num_feature, num_hidden]))
b1 = tf.Variable(tf.random_uniform([num_hidden]))

w2 = tf.Variable(tf.random_uniform([num_hidden, num_classes]))
b2 = tf.Variable(tf.random_uniform([num_classes]))
```

Then, we perform feedforward operation to predict the output, `Yhat`:

```
#layer 1
z1 = tf.matmul(X, w1) + b1
a1 = tf.nn.tanh(z1)

#output layer
z2 = tf.matmul(a1, w2) + b2
Yhat = tf.nn.tanh(z2)
```

We use mean squared error as our loss function:

```
loss_function = tf.reduce_mean(tf.square(Yhat - Y))
```

We then minimize the loss using Adam optimizer:

```
optimizer = tf.train.AdamOptimizer(1e-2).minimize(loss_function)
```

We initialize the TensorFlow variables:

```
init = tf.global_variables_initializer()
```

Reptile

Now we'll see how can we find the optimal parameters of our neural network with Reptile.

First, we initialize the necessary variables:

```
#number of epochs i.e training iterations
num_epochs = 100

#number of samples i.e number of shots
num_samples = 50

#number of tasks
num_tasks = 2

#number of times we want to perform optimization
num_iterations = 10

#mini btach size
mini_batch = 10
```

Then, we start the TensorFlow session:

```
with tf.Session() as sess:
    sess.run(init)
```

For the number of epochs:

```
for e in range(num_epochs):
    #for each task in batch of tasks
    for task in range(num_tasks):
```

We get the initial parameters of the model:

```
old_w1, old_b1, old_w2, old_b2 = sess.run([w1, b1, w2, b2,])
```

Then, we sample x and y:

```
x_sample, y_sample = sample_points(num_samples)
```

For some k number of iterations, we perform optimization on the task:

```
for k in range(num_iterations):

    #get the minibatch x and y
    for i in range(0, num_samples, mini_batch):

        #sample mini batch of examples
        x_minibatch = x_sample[i:i+mini_batch]
```

```
        y_minibatch = y_sample[i:i+mini_batch]


        train = sess.run(optimizer, feed_dict={X:
x_minibatch.reshape(mini_batch,1),
                                       Y:
y_minibatch.reshape(mini_batch,1)})
```

We get the updated model parameters after several iterations of optimization:

```
new_w1, new_b1, new_w2, new_b2 = sess.run([w1, b1, w2, b2])
```

Now, we perform the meta update:

```
epsilon = 0.1

updated_w1 = old_w1 + epsilon * (new_w1 - old_w1)
updated_b1 = old_b1 + epsilon * (new_b1 - old_b1)

updated_w2 = old_w2 + epsilon * (new_w2 - old_w2)
updated_b2 = old_b2 + epsilon * (new_b2 - old_b2)
```

We update the model parameter with new parameters:

```
w1.load(updated_w1, sess)
b1.load(updated_b1, sess)

w2.load(updated_w2, sess)
b2.load(updated_b2, sess)
```

Then, we print the loss for every 10 epochs:

```
if e%10 == 0:
    loss = sess.run(loss_function, feed_dict={X:
x_sample.reshape(num_samples,1), Y: y_sample.reshape(num_samples,1)})

    print "Epoch {}: Loss {}\n".format(e,loss)
    print 'Updated Model Parameter Theta\n'
    print 'Sampling Next Batch of Tasks \n'
    print '---------------------------------\n'
```

The complete code is given as follows:

```
#start the tensorflow session
with tf.Session() as sess:
    sess.run(init)
    for e in range(num_epochs):
        #for each task in batch of tasks
        for task in range(num_tasks):
```

```
          #get the initial parameters of the model
          old_w1, old_b1, old_w2, old_b2 = sess.run([w1, b1, w2, b2,])

          #sample x and y
          x_sample, y_sample = sample_points(num_samples)


          #for some k number of iterations perform optimization on the
    task
          for k in range(num_iterations):

              #get the minibatch x and y
              for i in range(0, num_samples, mini_batch):

                  #sample mini batch of examples
                  x_minibatch = x_sample[i:i+mini_batch]
                  y_minibatch = y_sample[i:i+mini_batch]


                  train = sess.run(optimizer, feed_dict={X:
    x_minibatch.reshape(mini_batch,1),
                                                         Y:
    y_minibatch.reshape(mini_batch,1)})

          #get the updated model parameters after several iterations of
    optimization
          new_w1, new_b1, new_w2, new_b2 = sess.run([w1, b1, w2, b2])

          #Now we perform meta update

          #i.e theta = theta + epsilon * (theta_star - theta)

          epsilon = 0.1

          updated_w1 = old_w1 + epsilon * (new_w1 - old_w1)
          updated_b1 = old_b1 + epsilon * (new_b1 - old_b1)

          updated_w2 = old_w2 + epsilon * (new_w2 - old_w2)
          updated_b2 = old_b2 + epsilon * (new_b2 - old_b2)


          #update the model parameter with new parameters
          w1.load(updated_w1, sess)
          b1.load(updated_b1, sess)

          w2.load(updated_w2, sess)
          b2.load(updated_b2, sess)
```

```
        if e%10 == 0:
            loss = sess.run(loss_function, feed_dict={X:
x_sample.reshape(num_samples,1), Y: y_sample.reshape(num_samples,1)})

            print "Epoch {}: Loss {}\n".format(e,loss)
            print 'Updated Model Parameter Theta\n'
            print 'Sampling Next Batch of Tasks \n'
            print '-------------------------------\n'
```

You can see the output as follows:

```
Epoch 0: Loss 13.0675544739

Updated Model Parameter Theta

Sampling Next Batch of Tasks


-------------------------------

Epoch 10: Loss 7.3604927063

Updated Model Parameter Theta

Sampling Next Batch of Tasks


-------------------------------

Epoch 20: Loss 4.35141277313

Updated Model Parameter Theta

Sampling Next Batch of Tasks


-------------------------------
```

Summary

In this chapter, we've learned about Meta-SGD and the Reptile algorithm. We saw how Meta-SGD differs from MAML and how Meta-SGD is used in supervised and reinforcement learning settings. We saw how Meta-SGD learns the model parameter along with learning rate and update direction. We also saw how to build Meta-SGD from scratch. Then, we learned about the Reptile algorithm. We saw how Reptile differs from MAML and how Reptile acts as an improvement over the MAML algorithm. We also learned how to use Reptile in a sine wave regression task.

In the next chapter, we'll learn how we can use gradient agreement as an optimization objective in meta learning.

Questions

1. How does Meta-SGD differ from MAML?
2. How does Meta-SGD find the optimal learning rate?
3. What is the update equation of the learning rate in meta-SGD?
4. How does the Reptile algorithm work?
5. What is the update equation of the Reptile algorithm?

Further readings

- Meta-SGD: https://arxiv.org/pdf/1707.09835.pdf
- Reptile: https://arxiv.org/pdf/1803.02999.pdf

8
Gradient Agreement as an Optimization Objective

In the last chapter, we learned about the Meta-SGD and Reptile algorithm. We saw how Meta-SGD is used to find the optimal parameter, optimal learning rate, and the gradient update direction. We also saw how the Reptile algorithm works and how it is more efficient than MAML. In this chapter, we'll learn how gradient agreement is used as an optimization objective for meta learning. As you saw in MAML, we were basically taking an average of gradients across tasks and updating our model parameter. In gradient agreement algorithm, we'll take a weighted average of gradients to update a model parameter and we'll see how adding weights to the gradient helps us to find the better model parameter. We'll explore exactly how gradient agreement algorithm work in this chapter. Our gradient agreement algorithm can be plugged with both MAML and the Reptile algorithm. We'll also see how to implement gradient agreement in MAML from scratch.

In this chapter, we'll learn about the following:

- Gradient agreement
- Weight calculation
- The gradient agreement algorithm
- Building gradient agreement algorithm with MAML

Gradient agreement as an optimization

The gradient agreement algorithm is an interesting and recently introduced algorithm that acts as an enhancement to meta learning algorithms. In MAML and Reptile, we try to find a better model parameter that's generalizable across several related tasks so that we can learn quickly with fewer data points. If we recollect what we've learned in the previous chapters, we've seen that we randomly initialize the model parameter and then we sample a random batch of tasks, T_i from the task distribution, $p(T)$. For each of the sampled tasks, T_i, we minimize the loss by calculating gradients and we get the updated parameters, θ'_i, and that forms our inner loop:

$$\theta'_i = \theta - \alpha \nabla_\theta L_{T_i}(f_\theta)$$

After calculating the optimal parameter for each of the sampled tasks, we perform meta optimization— that is, we perform meta optimization by calculating loss in a new set of tasks, we minimize loss by calculating gradients with respect to the optimal parameters θ'_i, which we obtained in the inner loop, and we update our initial model parameter θ:

$$\theta = \theta - \beta \nabla_\theta \sum_{T_i \sim p(T)} L_{T_i}(f_{\theta_i})$$

What's really going in the previous equation? If you closely examine this equation, you'll notice that we're merely taking an average of gradients across tasks and updating our model parameter θ, which implies all tasks contribute equally in updating our model parameter.

But what's wrong with this? Let's say we've sampled four tasks, and three tasks have a gradient update in one direction, but one task has a gradient update in a direction that completely differs from the other tasks. This disagreement can have a serious impact on updating the model's initial parameter since the gradient of all of the tasks contributes equally in updating the model parameter. As you can see in the following diagram, all tasks from T_1 to T_3 have a gradient in one direction but task T_4 has a gradient in a completely different direction compared to the other tasks:

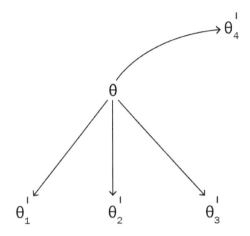

So, what should we do now? How can we understand which task has a strong gradient agreement and which tasks have a strong disagreement? If we associate weights with the gradients, can we understand the importance? So, we rewrite our outer gradient update equation by adding the weights multiplied with each of the gradients as follows:

$$\theta = \theta - \beta \sum_{i} w_i \nabla L_{T_i}\left(f_{\theta_i}\right)$$

Okay, how do we calculate these weights? These weights are proportional to the inner product of the gradients of a task and an average of gradients of all of the tasks in the sampled batch of tasks. But what does this imply?

It implies that **if the gradient of a task is in the same direction as the average gradient of all tasks in a sampled batch of tasks, then we can increase its weights so that it'll contribute more in updating our model parameter. Similarly, if the gradient of a task is in the direction that's greatly different from the average gradient of all tasks in a sampled batch of tasks, then we can decrease its weights so that it'll contribute less in updating our model parameter**. We'll see how exactly these weights are computed in the following section.

We can not only apply our gradient agreement algorithm to MAML, but also to the Reptile algorithm. So, our Reptile update equation becomes as follows:

$$\theta = \theta + \alpha \sum_{i} w_i\left(\theta_i' - \theta\right)$$

Weight calculation

We've seen that, by associating weights with the gradients, we can understand which tasks have strong gradient agreement and which tasks have strong gradient disagreement.

We know that these weights are proportional to the inner product of the gradients of a task and an average of gradients of all of the tasks in the sampled batch of tasks. How can we calculate these weights?

The weights are calculated as follows:

$$w_i = \frac{\sum_{j \in T}(g_i^T g_j)}{\sum_{k \in T} \left| \sum_{j \in T}(g_k^T g^j) \right|}$$

Let's say we sampled a batch of tasks. Then, for each task in a batch, we sample k data points, calculate loss, update the gradients, and find the optimal parameter θ'_i for each of the tasks. Along with this, we also store the gradient update vector of each task in g_i. It can be calculated as $g_i = \theta - \theta'_i$.

So, the weights for an ith task is the sum of the inner products of g_i and g_j divided by a normalization factor. The normalization factor is proportional to the inner product of g_i and $g_{average}$.

Let's better understand how these weights are calculated exactly by looking at the following code:

```
for i in range(num_tasks):
    g = theta - theta_[i]

#calculate normalization factor
normalization_factor = 0

for i in range(num_tasks):
    for j in range(num_tasks):
        normalization_factor += np.abs(np.dot(g[i].T, g[j]))

#calcualte weights
w = np.zeros(num_tasks)

for i in range(num_tasks):
    for j in range(num_tasks):
        w[i] += np.dot(g[i].T, g[j])

    w[i] = w[i] / normalization_factor
```

Algorithm

Now let's see how gradient agreement works step by step:

1. Let's say we have a model f parameterized by a parameter θ and a distribution over tasks $p(T)$. First, we randomly initialize the model parameter θ.

2. We sample some batch of tasks T_i from a distribution of tasks—that is, $T_i \sim p(T)$. Let's say we sampled two tasks, then $T = \{T_1, T_2\}$.

3. **Inner loop:** For each task (T_i) in tasks (T), we sample k data points and prepare our train and test datasets:

$$D_i^{train} = \{(x_1, y_1), (x_2, y_2). \ldots (x_k, y_k)\}$$

$$D_i^{test} = \{(x_1, y_1), (x_2, y_2). \ldots (x_k, y_k)\}$$

We calculate loss and minimize the loss on the D_i^{train} using gradient descent and get the optimal parameters θ_i'—that is, $\theta_i' = \theta - \alpha \nabla_\theta L_{T_i}(f_\theta)$.

Along with this, we also store the gradient update vector as: $g_i = \theta - \theta_i'$.

So, for each of the tasks, we sample k data points and minimize the loss on the train set D_i^{train} and get the optimal parameters θ_i'. As we sampled two tasks, we'll have two optimal parameters, $\theta' = \{\theta_1', \theta_2'\}$, and we'll have a gradient update vector for each of these two tasks as $g = \{(\theta - \theta_1'), (\theta - \theta_2')\}$.

4. **Outer loop:** Now, before performing meta optimization, we'll calculate the weights as follows:

$$w_i = \frac{\sum_{j \in T}(g_i^T g_j)}{\sum_{k \in T} |\sum_{j \in T}(g_k^T g^j)|}$$

After calculating the weights, we now perform meta optimization by associating the weights with the gradients. We minimize the loss in the D_i^{test} by calculating gradients with respect to the parameters obtained in the previous step and multiply the gradients with the weights.

If our meta learning algorithm is MAML, then the update equation is as follows:

$$\theta = \theta - \beta \sum_i w_i \nabla L_{T_i}(f_{\theta_i})$$

If our meta learning algorithm is Reptile, then the update equation is as follows:

$$\theta = \theta + \alpha \sum_i w_i (\theta' - \theta)$$

5. We repeat steps 2 to 5 for n number of iterations.

Building gradient agreement algorithm with MAML

In the last section, we saw how the gradient agreement algorithm works. We saw how gradient agreement adds weights to the gradients implying their importance. Now, we'll see how to use our gradient agreement algorithm with MAML by coding them from scratch using NumPy. For better understanding, we'll consider a simple binary classification task. We'll randomly generate our input data, train it with a simple single-layer neural network, and try to find the optimal parameter θ.

Now we'll see step by step exactly how to do this.

You can also check out the whole code, available as a Jupyter Notebook here: https://github.com/sudharsan13296/Hands-On-Meta-Learning-With-Python/blob/master/08.%20Gradient%20Agreement%20As%20An%20Optimization%20Objective/8.4%20Building%20Gradient%20Agreement%20Algorithm%20with%20MAML.ipynb.

We import all of the necessary libraries:

```
import numpy as np
```

Generating data points

Now, we define a function called `sample_points` for generating our input *(x,y)* pairs. It takes the parameter k as input, which implies the number of *(x,y)* pairs we want to sample:

```
def sample_points(k):
    x = np.random.rand(k,50)
    y = np.random.choice([0, 1], size=k, p=[.5, .5]).reshape([-1,1])
    return x,y
```

Single layer neural network

For simplicity and better understanding, we use a neural network with only a single layer for predicting the output:

```
a = np.matmul(X, theta)
YHat = sigmoid(a)
```

So, we use gradient agreement with MAML to find this optimal parameter value `theta` that is generalizable across tasks. This is so that, for a new task, we can learn from a few data points in less time by taking fewer gradient steps.

Gradient agreement in MAML

Now, we'll define a class called `GradientAgreement_MAML`, where we'll implement the gradient agreement MAML algorithm. In the __init__ method, we'll initialize all of the necessary variables. Then, we'll define our sigmoid activation function. Following this, we'll define our `train` function.

Let's see this step by step and we'll see the overall code:

```
class GradientAgreement_MAML(object):
```

We define the __init__ method and initialize all variables:

```
    def __init__(self):
        #initialize number of tasks i.e number of tasks we need in each
    batch of tasks
        self.num_tasks = 2
        #number of samples i.e number of shots -number of data points (k)
    we need to have in each task
        self.num_samples = 10
```

```
        #number of epochs i.e training iterations
        self.epochs = 100
        #hyperparameter for the inner loop (inner gradient update)
        self.alpha = 0.0001
        #hyperparameter for the outer loop (outer gradient update) i.e meta
optimization
        self.beta = 0.0001
        #randomly initialize our model parameter theta
        self.theta =
np.random.normal(size=self.pol_ord).reshape(self.pol_ord, 1)
```

Now, we define a function called `sigmoid` for converting our x into polynomial form:

```
    def sigmoid(self,a):
        return 1.0 / (1 + np.exp(-a))
```

Now, let's define a function called `train` for training:

```
    def train(self):
```

For the number of epochs, we do the following:

```
        for e in range(self.epochs):
            self.theta_ = []
            #for storing gradient updates
            self.g = []
```

For task `i` in a batch of tasks, we do the following:

```
            for i in range(self.num_tasks):
```

We sample k data points and prepare our train set, D_i^{train}:

```
            XTrain, YTrain = sample_points(self.num_samples)
```

We predict the value of `YHat`:

```
            a = np.matmul(XTrain, self.theta)

            YHat = self.sigmoid(a)
```

We calculate loss and minimize the loss using gradient descent, $\theta'_i = \theta - \alpha \nabla_\theta L_{T_i}(f_\theta)$:

```
                #since we're performing classification, we use cross
entropy loss as our loss function
                loss = ((np.matmul(-YTrain.T, np.log(YHat)) - np.matmul((1
-YTrain.T), np.log(1 - YHat)))/self.num_samples)[0][0]
                #minimize the loss by calculating gradients
                gradient = np.matmul(XTrain.T, (YHat - YTrain)) /
```

```
self.num_samples
```

```
                #update the gradients and find the optimal parameter theta'
for each of tasks
                self.theta_.append(self.theta - self.alpha*gradient)
```

We store the gradient updates in g, $g_i = \theta - \theta'_i$:

```
                self.g.append(self.theta-self.theta_[i])
```

Now, we calculate weights, $\quad w_i = \dfrac{\sum_{j \in T}(g_i^T\, g_j)}{\sum_{k \in T}|\sum_{j \in T}(g_k^T\, g^j)|}$:

```
            normalization_factor = 0
            for i in range(self.num_tasks):
                for j in range(self.num_tasks):
                    normalization_factor += np.abs(np.dot(self.g[i].T,
self.g[j]))
            w = np.zeros(self.num_tasks)
            for i in range(self.num_tasks):

                for j in range(self.num_tasks):
                    w[i] += np.dot(self.g[i].T, self.g[j])

                w[i] = w[i] / normalization_factor
```

We initialize weighted meta gradients:

```
            weighted_gradient = np.zeros(self.theta.shape)
```

For the number of tasks, we sample k data points and prepare our test set, D_i^{test}:

```
            for i in range(self.num_tasks):

                #sample k data points and prepare our test set for meta
training
                XTest, YTest = sample_points(10)
```

We predict the value of y:

```
                a = np.matmul(XTest, self.theta_[i])
                YPred = self.sigmoid(a)
```

We compute meta gradients:

```
meta_gradient = np.matmul(XTest.T, (YPred - YTest)) /
self.num_samples
```

Multiply the weights to the computed meta gradients and update the value of θ, using

$$\theta = \theta - \beta \sum_i w_i \nabla L_{T_i}\left(f_{\theta_i}\right)$$

:

```
weighted_gradient += np.sum(w[i]*meta_gradient)
    self.theta = self.theta-
self.beta*weighted_gradient/self.num_tasks
```

We print the loss for every 10 epochs:

```
if e%10==0:
    print "Epoch {}: Loss {}\n".format(e,loss)
    print 'Updated Model Parameter Theta\n'
    print 'Sampling Next Batch of Tasks \n'
    print '-----------------------------------\n'
```

The following is the whole class for GradientAgreement_MAML:

```
class GradientAgreement_MAML(object):
    def __init__(self):
        #initialize number of tasks i.e number of tasks we need in each
batch of tasks
        self.num_tasks = 2
        #number of samples i.e number of shots -number of data points (k)
we need to have in each task
        self.num_samples = 10

        #number of epochs i.e training iterations
        self.epochs = 100
        #hyperparameter for the inner loop (inner gradient update)
        self.alpha = 0.0001
        #hyperparameter for the outer loop (outer gradient update) i.e meta
optimization
        self.beta = 0.0001
        #randomly initialize our model parameter theta
        self.theta = np.random.normal(size=50).reshape(50, 1)
    #define our sigmoid activation function
    def sigmoid(self,a):
        return 1.0 / (1 + np.exp(-a))
    #now Let's get to the interesting part i.e training :P
    def train(self):
```

```
#for the number of epochs,
for e in range(self.epochs):
    self.theta_ = []
    #for storing gradient updates
    self.g = []
    #for task i in batch of tasks
    for i in range(self.num_tasks):
        #sample k data points and prepare our train set
        XTrain, YTrain = sample_points(self.num_samples)
        a = np.matmul(XTrain, self.theta)

        YHat = self.sigmoid(a)

        #since we're performing classification, we use cross
entropy loss as our loss function
        loss = ((np.matmul(-YTrain.T, np.log(YHat)) - np.matmul((1
-YTrain.T), np.log(1 - YHat)))/self.num_samples)[0][0]
        #minimize the loss by calculating gradients
        gradient = np.matmul(XTrain.T, (YHat - YTrain)) /
self.num_samples

        #update the gradients and find the optimal parameter theta'
for each of tasks
        self.theta_.append(self.theta - self.alpha*gradient)
        #compute the gradient update
        self.g.append(self.theta-self.theta_[i])
    #now we calculate the weights
    #we know that weight is the sum of dot product of g_i and g_j
divided by a normalization factor.
    normalization_factor = 0
    for i in range(self.num_tasks):
        for j in range(self.num_tasks):
            normalization_factor += np.abs(np.dot(self.g[i].T,
self.g[j]))
    w = np.zeros(self.num_tasks)
    for i in range(self.num_tasks):

        for j in range(self.num_tasks):
            w[i] += np.dot(self.g[i].T, self.g[j])

        w[i] = w[i] / normalization_factor
    #initialize meta gradients
    weighted_gradient = np.zeros(self.theta.shape)
    for i in range(self.num_tasks):
        #sample k data points and prepare our test set for meta
training
        XTest, YTest = sample_points(10)
```

```
                #predict the value of y
                a = np.matmul(XTest, self.theta_[i])
                YPred = self.sigmoid(a)
                #compute meta gradients
                meta_gradient = np.matmul(XTest.T, (YPred - YTest)) /
        self.num_samples
                weighted_gradient += np.sum(w[i]*meta_gradient)


            #update our randomly initialized model parameter theta with the
        meta gradients
            self.theta = self.theta-
        self.beta*weighted_gradient/self.num_tasks
            if e%10==0:
                print "Epoch {}: Loss {}\n".format(e,loss)
                print 'Updated Model Parameter Theta\n'
                print 'Sampling Next Batch of Tasks \n'
                print '---------------------------------\n'
```

We create an instance to our `GradientAgreement_MAML` class:

```
model = GradientAgreement_MAML()
```

Then, we train the model:

```
model.train()
```

You can see how the loss decreases over epochs:

```
Epoch 0: Loss 5.9436043239

Updated Model Parameter Theta

Sampling Next Batch of Tasks

---------------------------------

Epoch 10: Loss 3.905350606769

Updated Model Parameter Theta

Sampling Next Batch of Tasks

---------------------------------

Epoch 20: Loss 2.0736155578

Updated Model Parameter Theta
```

```
Sampling Next Batch of Tasks

---------------------------------

Epoch 30: Loss 1.48478751777

Updated Model Parameter Theta

Sampling Next Batch of Tasks

---------------------------------
```

Summary

In this chapter, we've learned about gradient agreement algorithm. We've seen how the gradient agreement algorithm uses a weighted gradient to find the better initial model parameter, θ. We also saw how these weights are proportional to the inner product of the gradients of a task and an average of gradients of all of the tasks in a sampled batch of tasks. We also explored how the gradient agreement algorithm can be plugged with both MAML and the Reptile algorithm. Following this, we saw how to find the optimal parameter θ in a classification task using a gradient agreement algorithm.

In the next chapter, we'll learn about some of the recent advancements in meta learning such as task agnostic meta learning, learning to learn in the concept space, and meta imitation learning.

Questions

1. What is gradient agreement and disagreement?
2. What is the update equation of MAML in gradient agreement?
3. What are the weights in gradient agreement?
4. How weights are computed?
5. What is a normalization factor?
6. When do we increase and decrease weights?

Further reading

- Gradient agreement algorithm paper: https://arxiv.org/pdf/1810.08178.pdf

9
Recent Advancements and Next Steps

Congratulations! We've made it to the final chapter. We've come a long way. We started off with meta learning fundamentals and then we saw several one-shot learning algorithms such as siamese, prototypical, matching, and relation networks. Later, we also saw how NTM stores and retrieves information. Going ahead, we saw interesting meta learning algorithms such as MAML, Reptile, and Meta-SGD. We saw how these algorithms find an optimal initial parameter. Now, we'll see some of the recent advancements in meta learning. We'll learn about how task agnostic meta learning is used for reducing task bias in meta learning and how meta learning is used in the imitation learning system. Then, we'll see how can we apply MAML in an unsupervised learning setting using the CACTUs algorithm. Later, we'll learn about a deep meta learning algorithm called learning to learn in the concept space.

In this chapter, you'll learn about the following:

- Task-agnostic meta-learning (TAML)
- Meta imitation learning
- CACTUs
- Learning to learn in the concept space

Task agnostic meta learning (TAML)

We know that, in meta learning, we train the model over a distribution of related tasks so that it can easily be adapted to a new task with only a few samples. In the previous chapters, we've seen how MAML finds the optimal initial parameters of the model by calculating meta gradients and performing meta optimization. But one of the problems we might face is that our model can be biased over some tasks, especially the tasks that are sampled in the meta training phase. So, our model will overperform on these tasks. If the model does so, then it will also lead us to the problem of finding a better update rule. With the biased model over some tasks, we'll also not able to perform better generalization on the unseen tasks that vary greatly from the meta training tasks.

To mitigate this, we need to make our model not get biased or overperform on some of the tasks. That is, we need to make our model task-agnostic, so that we can prevent task bias and attain better generalization. Now, we'll see two algorithms to perform TAML:

- Entropy maximization/reduction
- Inequality minimization

Entropy maximization/reduction

In this section, we'll see how can we prevent task bias by maximizing and minimizing entropy. We know that entropy is a measure of randomness. So, we maximize entropy by allowing the model to make a random guess over the predicted labels with equal probability. By making random guesses over the predicted label, we can prevent task bias.

How do we compute the entropy? Let's denote entropy by H. The entropy for T_i is computed by sampling x_i from $p_{T_i}(x_i)$ over its output probabilities, $y_{i,n}$ over N predicted labels:

$$H_{T_i}(f_\theta) = -\mathbb{E}_{x_i \sim P_{T_i}(x)} \sum_{n=1}^{N} \hat{y}_i, n log(\hat{y}_i, n)$$

In the previous equation, $\hat{y}_i$ is the predicted label by the model.

So, we maximize the entropy before updating the model parameter. Next, we minimize the entropy after updating the model parameter. So, what do we mean by minimizing the entropy? Minimizing the entropy implies that we don't add any randomness over the predicted labels and we allow the model to predict the label with high confidence.

So, our goal is to maximize the entropy reduction for each of the tasks and it can be represented as follows:

$$H_{T_i}(f_\theta) - H_{T_i}(f_{\theta_i})$$

We incorporate our entropy term with the meta objective and try to find the optimal parameter θ, so our meta objective becomes the following:

$$\theta = \theta - \beta \nabla_\theta \{ \mathbb{E}_{T_i \sim p(T)} L_{T_i}(f_{\theta_i'}) + \lambda[-H_{T_i}(f_\theta) + H_{T_i}(f_{\theta_i})] \}$$

And λ is the balancing coefficient between both of these terms.

Algorithm

Now, we'll see how entropy TAML works step by step:

1. Let's say we've a model f parameterized by a parameter θ and we've a distribution over tasks $p(T)$. First, we randomly initialize the model parameter, θ.

2. Sample a batch of tasks from a distribution of tasks—that is, $T_i \sim p(T)$. Say, we've sampled three tasks then: $T = \{T_1, T_2, T_3\}$.

3. **Inner loop**: For each task (T_i) in tasks (T), we sample k data points and prepare our train and test datasets:

$$D_{train} = \{(x_1, y_1), (x_2, y_2) \ldots (x_k, y_k)\}$$

$$D'_{test} = \{(x'_1, y'_1), (x'_2, y'_2) \ldots (x'_k, y'_k)\}$$

Then, we calculate the loss on our training set D_{train}, minimize the loss using gradient descent, and get the optimal parameters:

$$\theta_i' = \theta - \alpha \nabla_\theta L_{T_i}$$

So, for each of the tasks, we sample k data points, prepare the train dataset, minimize the loss, and get the optimal parameters. Since we sampled three tasks, we'll have three optimal parameters: $\theta' = \{\theta_1', \theta_2', \theta_3'\}$.

4. **Outer loop**: We perform meta optimization. Here, we try to minimize the loss on our meta training set, D_{test_i}. We minimize the loss by calculating the gradient with respect to our optimal parameter θ'_i and update our randomly initialized parameter θ; along with this, we'll add the entropy term. So our final meta objective becomes the following:

$$\theta = \theta - \beta\nabla_\theta \{\mathbb{E}_{T_i \sim p(T)} L_{T_i}(f_{\theta'_i}) + \lambda[-H_{T_i}(f_\theta) + H_{T_i}(f_{\theta_i})]\}$$

5. We repeat steps 2 to 4 for n number of iterations.

Inequality minimization

The problem with the entropy method is that it's applicable only to classification tasks. So, we can't apply our algorithm for regression or reinforcement learning tasks. To overcome this, we'll see one more algorithm, called inequality minimization TAML. It's as simple as the entropy method. In this method, we try to minimize the inequality. There are several inequality measures used in economics to measure income distribution, wealth distribution, and more. In our meta learning setting, we can use these economic inequality measures to minimize our task bias. So, the bias of the model toward a task can be minimized by minimizing the inequality over the losses of all of the sampled tasks in a batch.

Inequality measures

We'll see some of the commonly used inequality measures. We can define our loss in the task T_i as l_i, the mean loss over the sampled tasks as $\bar{l}$, and the number of tasks in a single batch as M.

Gini coefficient

It's one of the most widely used measures of inequality. It measures the inequality of a distribution using a Lorenz curve. A Lorenz curve is a cumulative frequency curve that compares the distribution of a specific variable with a uniform distribution that represents the equality. The value of a Gini coefficient ranges from 0 to 1, where 0 represents perfect equality and the value of 1 perfects inequality. It's basically half of the relative absolute mean difference.

So, in our meta learning setting, we can calculate the Gini coefficient as follows:

$$G = \frac{\sum_{i=1}^{M} \sum_{j=1}^{M} |l_i - l_j|}{2n \sum \sum_{i=1}^{M} l_i}$$

Theil index

The Theil index is another commonly used inequality measure. It's named after a Dutch econometrician, Henri Theil, and it's a special case of the family of inequality measures called **generalized entropy measures**. It can be defined as the difference between the maximum entropy and observed entropy.

We calculate the Theil index for our meta learning setting as follows:

$$T = \frac{1}{M} \sum_{i=1}^{M} \frac{l_i}{l} \ln \frac{l_i}{l}$$

Variance of algorithms

The variance of algorithms can be defined as follows:

$$V_L(l) = \frac{1}{M} \sum_{i=1}^{M} [\ln l_i - \ln g(l)]^2$$

In the previous equation, $g(l)$ implies the geometric mean of l.

We can use any of these inequality measures to calculate the task bias. So, once we calculate the task bias using this inequality measure, we can minimize the bias by plugging our inequality measure into the meta objective. So, we can rewrite our meta objective as follows:

$$\theta - \beta \nabla_\theta [\mathbb{E}_{T_i \sim p(T)} L_{T_i}(f_{\theta'_i}) + \lambda I(L_{T_i}(f_{\theta'_i}))]$$

In the previous equation, $I(L_{T_i}(f_{\theta'_i}))$ represents our inequality measure and λ is the balancing coefficient.

Algorithm

Now, we'll see how inequality minimization TAML works step by step:

1. Let's say we have a model f parameterized by a parameter θ and we've a distribution over tasks $p(T)$. First, we randomly initialize the model parameter θ.

2. We sample a batch of tasks from a distribution of tasks—that is, $T_i \sim p(T)$. Say, we've sampled three tasks, then $T = \{T_1, T_2, T_3\}$.

3. **Inner loop**: For each task (T_i) in tasks (T), we sample k data points and prepare our train and test datasets:

$$D_{train} = \{(x_1, y_1), (x_2, y_2)\ldots\ldots(x_k, y_k)\}$$

$$D'_{test} = \{(x'_1, y'_1), (x'_2, y'_2)\ldots\ldots(x'_k, y'_k)\}$$

Then, we calculate the loss on the our training set D_{train}, minimize the loss using gradient descent, and get the optimal parameters:

$$\theta'_i = \theta - \alpha \nabla_\theta L_{T_i}$$

So, for each of the tasks, we sample k data points, prepare the train dataset, minimize the loss, and get the optimal parameters. Since we sampled three tasks, we'll have three optimal parameters—that is, $\theta' = \{\theta'_1, \theta'_2, \theta'_3\}$.

4. **Outer loop**: Now, we perform meta optimization. Here, we try to minimize the loss on our training set, D_{test_i}. We minimize the loss by calculating the gradient with respect to our optimal parameter θ'_i and update our randomly initialized parameter θ; along with this, we'll add the entropy term. So, our final meta objective becomes the following:

$$\theta = \theta - \beta \nabla_\theta [\mathbb{E}_{T_i \sim p(T)} L_{T_i}(f_{\theta'_i}) + \lambda\, I(L_{T_i}(f_{\theta'_i})]$$

5. We repeat steps 2 to 4 for n number of iterations.

Meta imitation learning

If we want our robot to be more generalist and to perform various tasks, then our robots should learn quickly. But how can we enable our robots to learn quickly? Well, how do we humans learn quickly? Don't we easily learn new skills by just looking at other individuals? Similarly, if we enable our robot to learn by just looking at our actions, then we can easily make the robot learn complex goals efficiently and we don't have to engineer complex goal and reward functions. This type of learning—that is, learning from human actions—is called imitation learning, where the robot tries to mimic human action. A robot doesn't really have to learn only from human actions; it can also learn from another robot performing a task or a video of a human/robot performing a task.

But imitation learning is not as simple as it sounds. A robot will take a lot of time and demonstrations to learn the goal and to identify the right policy. So, we'll augment the robot with prior experience as demonstrations (training data) so that it doesn't have to learn each skill completely from scratch. Augmenting the robot with prior experience helps it to learn quickly. So, to learn several skills, we need to collect demonstrations for each of those skills—that is, we need to augment the robots with task-specific demonstration data.

But how can we enable our robot to learn quickly from a single demonstration for a task? Can we use meta learning here? Can we reuse the demonstration data and learn from several related tasks to learn the new task quickly? So, we combine meta learning and imitation learning and form **Meta Imitation Learning** (MIL). With MIL, we can make use of demonstration data from a variety of other tasks to learn a new task quickly with just one demonstration. So, we can find the right policy for a new task with just one demonstration of that task.

For MIL, we can use any of the meta learning algorithms we've seen. We'll use MAML as our meta learning algorithm, which is compatible with any algorithm that can be trained with gradient descent and we'll use policy gradients as our algorithm for finding the right policy. In policy gradients, we directly optimize the parameterized policy π_θ with some parameter θ.

Our goal is to learn a policy that can quickly adapt to new tasks from a single demonstration of that task. By doing so, we can remove our dependency on a large amount of demonstration data for each of the tasks. What is actually our task here? Our task will contain the trajectories. A trajectory tr consists of a sequence of observations and actions from the expert policy which is the demonstrations. Wait. What is an expert policy? Since we're performing imitation learning, we're learning from the experts (human actions) so we call that policy an expert policy and it's denoted by π^*:

$$trajectory = \{o_t, a_1, \ldots \ldots, o_t, a_t\} \sim \pi_i^*$$

Okay, what should our loss function be? The loss function denotes how our robot actions differ from the expert actions. We can use mean squared error loss as our loss function for continuous actions, and cross-entropy as a loss function for discrete actions. Let's say we have continuous actions; then we can represent our mean squared error loss as follows:

$$L_{T_i}(f_\theta) = \sum_{tr^{(j)} \sim T_i} \sum_t ||f_\theta(o_t)^{(j)} - a_t^{(j)}||_2^2$$

Say we have a distribution over tasks $p(T)$. We sample a batch of tasks and for each task T_i, we sample some demonstration data, train the network by minimizing the loss, and find the optimal parameter θ'. Next, we perform meta optimization by calculating meta gradients and find the optimal initial parameter θ. We'll see exactly how this works in the next section.

MIL algorithm

The steps involved in MIL are as follows:

1. Let's say we've a model f parameterized by a parameter θ and we've a distribution over tasks $p(T)$. First we randomly initialize the model parameter θ.
2. Sample some batch of tasks T_i from a distribution of tasks, that is, $T_i \sim p(T)$.
3. **Inner loop**: For each of the tasks in the sampled tasks, we sample a demonstration data—that is, $trajectory = \{o_1, a_1 \ldots o_t, a_t\}$. Now we compute loss and minimize the loss by performing gradient descent and we get the optimal parameters θ_i'—that is, $\theta_i' = \theta - \alpha \nabla_\theta L_{T_i}(f_\theta)$. Then, we also sample one more demonstration data for the meta training: $trajectory' = \{o_1', a_1' \ldots o_t', a_t'\}$.
4. **Outer loop**: Now we update our initial parameter using $trajectory'$ by meta optimization, as follows:

$$\theta = \theta - \beta \nabla_\theta \sum_{T_i \sim p(T)} L_{T_i}(f_{\theta_i'})$$

5. Repeat steps 2 to 4 for n number of iterations.

CACTUs

We've seen how MAML helps us to find the optimal initial model parameter so that we can generalize it to many other related tasks. We've also seen how MAML is used in supervised and reinforcement learning settings. But how can we apply MAML in an unsupervised learning setting where we don't have labels for our data points? So, we introduce a new algorithm called **CACTUS** short for **Clustering to Automatically Generate Tasks for Unsupervised Model Agnostic Meta Learning.**

Let's say we have a dataset D containing unlabeled examples: $D = \{x_1, x_2, x_3 \ldots x_n\}$. Now, what can we do with this dataset? How can we apply MAML over this dataset? First, what do we need for training using MAML? We need a distribution over tasks and we train our model by sampling a batch of tasks and find the optimal model parameter. A task should contain a feature along with its label. But how can we generate a task from our unlabeled dataset?

Let's see how can we generate tasks using CACTUS in the next section. Once we generate the tasks, we can plug them easily into the MAML algorithm and find the optimal model parameter.

Task generation using CACTUs

Let's say we've a dataset set D containing samples without labels: $D = \{x_1, x_2, x_3 \ldots x_n\}$. Now we need to create labels for our dataset. How can we do that? First, we learn the embeddings of each of the data points in our dataset using some embedding function. The embedding function can be any feature extractor. Say our input is an image, then we can use CNN as our embedding function for extracting an image feature vector.

After generating the embeddings for each of the data points, how can we find the labels for them? A naive and simple approach would be to partition our dataset D into some P partitions with some random hyperplanes and then we can treat each of these partitioned subsets of a dataset as a separate class.

But the problem with this method is that, since we're using random hyperplanes, our classes may contain completely different embeddings and it also keeps the related embeddings in different classes. So, instead of using random hyperplanes to partition our dataset, we can use a clustering algorithm. We use k-means clustering as our clustering algorithm to partition our dataset. We run k-means clustering for several iterations and get the k clusters (partitions).

We can treat each of these clusters as a separate class. So, what's next? How can we generate the task? Let's say that, as a result of clustering, we have five clusters. We sample n clusters from these five clusters. Then, we sample r data points from each of the n clusters without replacement; this can be represented as $\{x_r\}_n$. After that, we sample a permutation of n one-hot task-specific labels, l_n, for assigning labels for each of the n sampled clusters. So now we'll have a data point, $\{x_r\}_n$, and a label, l_n.

Finally, we can define our task T as $T = \{(x_{n,r}, l_n)|x_{n,r} \in \{x_r\}_n\}$.

Learning to learn in concept space

Now we'll see how to learn to learn in the concept space using deep meta learning. First, how do we perform meta learning? We sample a batch of related tasks and some k data points in each task and train our meta learner. Instead of just training using our vanilla meta learning technique, we can combine the power of deep learning with meta learning. So, when we sample a batch of tasks and some k data points in each task, we learn the representations of each of the k data points using deep neural networks and then we'll perform meta learning on those representations.

Our framework consists of three components:

- Concept generator
- Concept discriminator
- Meta learner

The role of the concept generator is to extract the feature representations of each of the data points in our dataset, capturing its high-level concept, and the role of the concept discriminator is to recognize and classify the concepts generated by the concept generator, while the meta learner learns on the concepts generated by the concept generator. All of the previous components—that is, the concept generator, concept discriminator, and meta learner—learn together. So, we improve the vanilla meta learning by integrating meta learning with deep learning. Our concept generator evolves with new incoming data so we can view our framework as a lifelong learning system.

But what's really going on here? Look at the following diagram; as you can see, we sample a set of tasks and feed them to our concept generator, which learns the concepts—that is, embeddings—and then feeds those concepts to the meta learner, which learns on these concepts and sends the loss back to the concept generator. Meanwhile, we also feed some external dataset to the concept generator, which learns the concepts for those inputs and sends those concepts to the concept discriminator. The concept discriminator predicts the labels for those concepts, calculates the loss, and sends the loss back to the concept generator. By doing so, we enhance our concept generator's ability to generalize concepts:

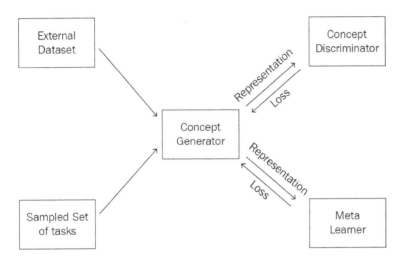

But still, why are we doing this? Instead of performing meta learning on a raw dataset, we perform meta learning in the concept space. How do we learn these concepts? These concepts are generated by the concept generator by learning the embeddings of the input. So, we train the concept generator and meta learner on various related tasks; along with this, we improve the concept generator through the concept discriminator by feeding an external dataset to the concept generator so that it can learn the concepts better. This joint training process allows our concept generator to learn various concepts and perform better on related tasks; we feed the external dataset only to enhance the performance of our concept generator, which learns continuously when we feed a new set of inputs. So, it's a lifelong learning system.

Key components

Now let's see each of our components in detail.

Concept generator

As we know, a concept generator is used to extract features. We can use deep neural nets parameterized by some parameter θ_G for generating the concepts. For examples, our concept generator can be a CNN if our input is an image.

Concept discriminator

It's basically a classifier and is used to predict the labels for the concepts generated by the concept generator. So it can be any of the supervised learning algorithms such as SVM and decision trees, parameterized by θ_D.

Meta learner

Our meta learner can be any meta learning algorithm, say MAML, Meta-SGD, or Reptile, parameterized by θ_M.

Loss function

We use two sets of loss functions here:

- Concept discrimination loss
- Meta learning loss

Concept discrimination loss

We sample some data points (x, y) from our dataset $\mathbb{D}$, feed them to the concept generator which learns the concepts and sends them to the concept discriminator, which tries to predict the classes for those concepts. So, the concept discriminator loss implies how good our concept discriminator is at predicting the classes and it can be represented as follows:

$$L_{(x,y)}(\theta_D, \theta_G)$$

Our loss function can be any loss function according to our task. For example, it can be a cross entropy loss if we're performing classification tasks.

Meta learning loss

We sample some batch of tasks from the task distributions, learn their concepts via the concept generator, perform meta learning on those concepts, and then we compute the meta learning loss:

$$L_T(\theta_M, \theta_G)$$

Our meta learning loss varies depending upon what meta learner we use, such as MAML or Reptile.

Our final loss function is a combination of both of these, concept discrimination and meta learning loss:

$$Loss = L_T(\theta_M, \theta_G) + \lambda L_{(x,y)}(\theta_D, \theta_G)$$

In the previous equation, lambda is a hyperparameter balancing between meta learning and concept discrimination loss. So, our objective becomes finding the optimal parameter that minimizes this loss:

$$min_{\theta_D, \theta_M, \theta_G} \mathbb{E}_{T \sim p(T), (x,y) \sim \mathbb{D}} J[L_T(\theta_M, \theta_G), L_{(x,y)}(\theta_D, \theta_G))]$$

We minimize the loss by calculating gradients and update our model parameters:

$$(\theta_D, \theta_M, \theta_G) = (\theta_D, \theta_M, \theta_G) - \beta \nabla [J(L_T(\theta_M, \theta_G), L_{(x,y)}(\theta_D, \theta_G))$$

Algorithm

Now we'll see how our algorithm works step by step:

1. Let's say we've a task distribution $p(T)$. First, we randomly initialize our model parameters such as a parameter of concept generator θ_G, meta learner θ_M, and concept discriminator θ_D.
2. We sample a batch of tasks from the task distributions and learn their concepts via the concept generator, perform meta learning on those concepts, and then compute the meta learning loss:

$$L_T(\theta_M, \theta_G)$$

3. We sample some data points (x, y) from our external dataset D, feed them to the concept generator to learn their concept, feed those concepts to the concept discriminator, which classifies them, and then we compute the concept discrimination loss:

$$L_{(x,y)}(\theta_D, \theta_G))$$

4. We combine both of these losses and try to minimize the loss using SGD and get the updated model parameters: $(\theta_D, \theta_M, \theta_G) = (\theta_D, \theta_M, \theta_G) - \beta \nabla [J(L_T(\theta_M, \theta_G), L_{(x,y)}(\theta_D, \theta_G))$.

5. Repeat steps 2 to 4 for n number of iterations.

Congratulations again for learning all of the important and popular meta learning algorithms. Meta learning is an interesting and most promising field of AI that will take us closer toward **Artificial General Intelligence (AGI)**. Now that you've finished reading this book, you can start exploring various advancements in meta learning and start experimenting with various projects. Learn and meta learn!

Summary

In this chapter, we've learned about TAML for reducing the task bias. We saw two types of methods: entropy-based and inequality-based TAML. Then, we explored meta imitation learning, which combines meta learning with imitation learning. We saw how meta learning helps imitation learning to learn from fewer imitations. We also saw how to apply model agnostic meta learning in an unsupervised learning setting using CACTUS. Then, we explored a deep meta learning algorithm called learning to learn in concept space. We saw how meta learning can be boosted by the power of deep learning.

Meta learning is one of the most interesting branches in the field of AI; now that you've understood various meta learning algorithms, you can start building meta learning models that are generalizable across various tasks and contribute to meta learning research.

Questions

1. What are all the different types of inequality measures?
2. What is called Theil index?
3. What is imitation learning?
4. What is a concept generator?
5. What is meta learning loss?

Further reading

- Task-Agnostic Meta-Learning: `https://arxiv.org/pdf/1805.07722.pdf`
- Meta imitation learning: `http://proceedings.mlr.press/v78/finn17a/finn17a.pdf`
- CACTUS: `https://arxiv.org/pdf/1810.02334.pdf`
- Learning to learn in the concept space: `https://arxiv.org/pdf/1802.03596.pdf`

Assessments

Chapter 1: Introduction to Meta Learning

1. Meta learning produces a versatile AI model that can learn to perform various tasks without having to be trained from scratch. We train our meta learning model on various related tasks with a few data points, so for a new but related task, the model can make use of what it learned from the previous tasks without having to be trained from scratch.

2. Learning from fewer data points is called **few-shot learning** or **k-shot learning**, where k denotes the number of data points in each of the classes in the dataset.

3. In order to make our model learn from a few data points, we will train it in the same way. So, when we have a dataset D, we sample some data points from each of the classes present in our dataset and we call it the support set.

4. We sample different data points from each of the classes that differ from the support set and call it the query set.

5. In a metric-based meta learning setting, we will learn the appropriate metric space. Let's say we want to find out the similarities between two images. In a metric-based setting, we use a simple neural network, which extracts the features from the two images and finds the similarities by computing the distance between the features of those two images.

6. We train our model in an **episodic fashion**; that is, in each episode, we sample a few data points from our dataset D, and prepare our support set and learn on the support set. So, over a series of episodes, our model will learn how to learn from a smaller dataset.

Chapter 2: Face and Audio Recognition Using Siamese Networks

1. A siamese network is a special type of neural network, and it is one of the simplest and most commonly used one-shot learning algorithms. Siamese networks basically consist of two symmetrical neural networks that share the same weights and architecture and are joined together at the end using an energy function, E.

2. The contrastive loss function can be expressed as follows:

$$Contrastive\ Loss = Y(E)^2 + (1-Y)max(margin - E, 0)^2$$

    In the preceding equation, the value of Y is the true label, which will be 1 when the two input values are similar and 0 if the two input values are dissimilar, and E is our energy function, which can be any distance measure. The term **margin** is used to hold the constraint; that is, when two input values are dissimilar and if their distance is greater than a margin, then they do not incur a loss.

3. The energy function tells us how similar the two inputs are. It is basically any similarity measure, such as Euclidean distance and cosine similarity.

4. The input to the siamese networks should be in pairs, (X_1, X_2), along with their binary label, $Y \in (0, 1)$, stating whether the input pairs are genuine pairs (the same) or imposite pairs (different).

5. The applications of siamese networks are endless; they've been stacked with various architectures for performing various tasks, such as human action recognition, scene change detection, and machine translation.

Chapter 3: Prototypical Networks and Their Variants

1. Prototypical networks are simple, efficient, and one of the most popularly used few-shot learning algorithms. The basic idea of the prototypical network is to create a prototypical representation of each class and classify a query point (new point) based on the distance between the class prototype and the query point.

2. We compute embeddings for each of the data points to learn the features.

3. Once we learn the embeddings of each data point, we take the mean embeddings of data points in each class and form the class prototype. So, a class prototype is basically the mean embeddings of data points in a class.

4. In a Gaussian prototypical network, along with generating embeddings for the data points, we add a confidence region around them, which is characterized by a Gaussian covariance matrix. Having a confidence region helps to characterize the quality of individual data points, and it is useful with noisy and less homogeneous data.

5. Gaussian prototypical networks differ from vanilla prototypical networks in that in a vanilla prototypical network, we learn only the embeddings of a data point, but in a Gaussian prototypical network, along with learning embeddings, we also add a confidence region to them.

6. The radius and diagonal are the different components of the covariance matrix used in a Gaussian prototypical network.

Chapter 4: Relation and Matching Networks Using TensorFlow

1. A relation network consists of two important functions: the embedding function, denoted by f_φ, and the relation function, denoted by g_ϕ.

2. Once we have the feature vectors of the support set, $f_\varphi(x_i)$, and query set, $f_\varphi(x_j)$, we combine them using an operator, Z. Here, Z can be any combination operator; we use concatenation as an operator to combine the feature vectors of the support set and the query set—that is, $Z(f_\varphi(x_i), f_\varphi(x_j))$.

3. The relation function, g_ϕ, will generate a relation score ranging from 0 to 1, representing the similarity between samples in the support set, x_i, and samples in the query set, x_j.

4. Our loss function can be represented as follows:

$$\varphi, \phi < -argmin_{\phi, \varphi} \sum_{i=1}^{m} \sum_{j=1}^{n} (r_{i,j} - 1(y_i == y_j))^2$$

5. In matching networks, we use two embedding functions, f and g, to learn the embeddings of the query set $\hat{x}$ and the support set x_i, respectively.

6. The output, $\hat{y}$, for the query point, $\hat{x}$, can be predicted as follows:

$$\hat{y} = \sum_{i=1}^{k} a(\hat{x}, x_i) y_i$$

Chapter 5: Memory-Augmented Neural Networks

1. NTM is an interesting algorithm that has the ability to store and retrieve information from memory. The idea of NTM is to augment the neural network with external memory—that is, instead of using hidden states as memory, it uses external memory to store and retrieve information.

2. The controller is basically a feed-forward neural network or recurrent neural network. It reads from and writes to memory.

3. The read head and write head are the pointers containing addresses of the memory that it has to read from and write to.

4. The memory matrix or memory bank, or simply the memory, is where we will store the information. Memory is basically a two-dimensional matrix composed of memory cells. The memory matrix contains N rows and M columns. Using the controller, we access the content from the memory. So, the controller receives input from the external environment and emits the response by interacting with the memory matrix.

5. Location-based addressing and content-based addressing are the different types of addressing mechanisms used in NTM.

6. An interpolation gate is used to decide whether we should use the weights we obtained at the previous time step, w_{t-1}, or use the weights obtained through content-based addressing, w_t^c.

7. Computing the least-used weight vector, w_t^{lu}, from the usage weight vector, w_t^u, is very simple. We simply set the index of the lowest value usage weight vector to 1 and the rest of the values to 0, as the lowest value in the usage weight vector means that it is least recently used.

Chapter 6: MAML and Its Variants

1. MAML is one of the recently introduced and most commonly used meta learning algorithms, and it has lead to a major breakthrough in meta learning research. The basic idea of MAML is to find better initial parameters so that, with good initial parameters, the model can learn quickly on new tasks with fewer gradient steps.

2. MAML is model agnostic, meaning that we can apply MAML for any models that are trainable with gradient descent.

3. ADML is a variant of MAML that makes use of both clean and adversarial samples to find the better and robust initial model parameter, θ.

4. In FGSM, we get the adversarial sample of our image and we calculate the gradients of our loss with respect to our image, more clearly input pixels of our image instead of the model parameter.

5. The context parameter is a task-specific parameter that's updated on the inner loop. It is denoted by ∅ and it is specific to each task and represents the embeddings of an individual task.

6. The shared parameter is shared across tasks and updated in the outer loop to find the optimal model parameter. It is denoted by θ.

Chapter 7: Meta-SGD and Reptile Algorithms

1. Unlike MAML, in Meta-SGD, along with finding optimal parameter value, θ, we also find the optimal learning rate, α, and update the direction.

2. The learning rate is implicitly implemented in the adaptation term. So, in Meta-SGD, we don't initialize a learning rate with a small scalar value. Instead, we initialize them with random values with the same shape as θ and learn them along with θ.

3. The update equation of the learning rate can be expressed as
$$\alpha = \alpha - \beta \nabla_\theta \sum_{T_i \sim p(T)} L_{T_i}(f_{\theta_i'})$$
.

4. Sample n tasks and run SGD for fewer iterations on each of the sampled tasks, and then update our model parameter in a direction that is common to all the tasks.

5. The reptile update equation can be expressed as $\theta = \theta + \epsilon(\theta' - \theta)$.

Chapter 8: Gradient Agreement as an Optimization Objective

1. When the gradients of all tasks are in the same direction, then it is called gradient agreement, and when the gradient of some tasks differ greatly from others, then it is called gradient disagreement.

2. The update equation in gradient agreement can be expressed as
$$\theta = \theta - \beta \sum_i w_i \nabla L_{T_i}(f_{\theta_i})$$
.

3. Weights are proportional to the inner product of the gradients of a task and the average of gradients of all of the tasks in the sampled batch of tasks.

4. The weights are calculated as follows:
$$w_i = \frac{\sum_{j \in T}(g_i^T g_j)}{\sum_{k \in T} |\sum_{j \in T}(g_k^T g^j)|}$$

5. The normalization factor is proportional to the inner product of g_i and $g_{average}$.

6. If the gradient of a task is in the same direction as the average gradient of all tasks in a sampled batch of tasks, then we can increase its weights so that it'll contribute more when updating our model parameter. Similarly, if the gradient of a task is in the direction that's greatly different from the average gradient of all tasks in a sampled batch of tasks, then we can decrease its weights so that it'll contribute less when updating our model parameter.

Chapter 9: Recent Advancements and Next Steps

1. Different types of inequality measures are Gini coefficients, the Theil index, and the variance of algorithms.

2. The Theil index is the most commonly used inequality measure. It's named after a Dutch econometrician, Henri Theil, and it's a special case of the family of inequality measures called **generalized entropy measures**. It can be defined as the difference between the maximum entropy and observed entropy.

3. If we enable our robot to learn by just looking at our actions, then we can easily make the robot learn complex goals efficiently and we don't have to engineer complex goal and reward functions. This type of learning—that is, learning from human actions—is called imitation learning, where the robot tries to mimic human action.

4. A concept generator is used to extract features. We can use deep neural nets that are parameterized by some parameter, θ_G, to generate the concepts. For examples, our concept generator can be a CNN if our input is an image.

5. We sample a batch of tasks from the task distributions, learn their concepts via the concept generator, perform meta learning on those concepts, and then we compute the meta learning loss:

$$L_T(\theta_M, \theta_G)$$

Other Books You May Enjoy

If you enjoyed this book, you may be interested in these other books by Packt:

Hands-On Transfer Learning with Python
Dipanjan Sarkar

ISBN: 9781788831307

- Set up your own DL environment with graphics processing unit (GPU) and Cloud support
- Delve into transfer learning principles with ML and DL models
- Explore various DL architectures, including CNN, LSTM, and capsule networks
- Learn about data and network representation and loss functions
- Get to grips with models and strategies in transfer learning
- Walk through potential challenges in building complex transfer learning models from scratch
- Explore real-world research problems related to computer vision and audio analysis
- Understand how transfer learning can be leveraged in NLP

Deep Reinforcement Learning Hands-On
Maxim Lapan

ISBN: 9781788834247

- Understand the DL context of RL and implement complex DL models
- Learn the foundation of RL: Markov decision processes
- Evaluate RL methods including Cross-entropy, DQN, Actor-Critic, TRPO, PPO, DDPG, D4PG and others
- Discover how to deal with discrete and continuous action spaces in various environments
- Defeat Atari arcade games using the value iteration method
- Create your own OpenAI Gym environment to train a stock trading agent
- Teach your agent to play Connect4 using AlphaGo Zero
- Explore the very latest deep RL research on topics including AI-driven chatbots

Leave a review - let other readers know what you think

Please share your thoughts on this book with others by leaving a review on the site that you bought it from. If you purchased the book from Amazon, please leave us an honest review on this book's Amazon page. This is vital so that other potential readers can see and use your unbiased opinion to make purchasing decisions, we can understand what our customers think about our products, and our authors can see your feedback on the title that they have worked with Packt to create. It will only take a few minutes of your time, but is valuable to other potential customers, our authors, and Packt. Thank you!

Index

R

rectified linear unit (ReLU) 29
Recurrent Neural Network (RNN) 11
relation networks
  about 68
  building, Tensorflow used 75, 77, 78
  in few-shot learning 71, 73, 74
  in one-shot learning 68, 69, 70
  in zero-shot learning 74
  loss function 75
Reptile algorithm
  about 162, 163
  implementing 166
  sine wave regression 164

S

semi prototypical networks 63, 64
siamese networks
  about 20
  applications 24
  architecture 22, 23
  audio recognition model, building 35, 36, 38, 39
  reference 24
  using, in face recognition 25, 26, 28, 29, 30, 32, 33
  working 20

sine wave regression, Reptile
  about 164
  data points generation 164
  two layered neural network 165
Stochastic Gradient Descent (SGD) 162
support set 9, 44
support set embedding function (g) 82

T

task generation
  with CACTUS 193
Task-agnostic meta-learning (TAML)
  about 186
  entropy maximization/reduction 186
  implementing 190
  inequality minimization 188
  working 187, 188
tasks
  copying, Neural Turing Machine (NTM) used 103, 105
TensorFlow
  matching networks 84, 86, 87
  relation networks, building 75, 77, 78
Theil index 189

Z

zero-shot learning 8

CPSIA information can be obtained
at www.ICGtesting.com
Printed in the USA
LVHW102350010519
616359LV00003B/81/P